METAPHOR

Metaphor is a central concept in literary studies, but it is also prevalent in everyday language and speech. Recent literary theories such as postmodernism and deconstruction have transformed the study of the text and revolutionised our thinking about metaphor.

In this illuminating volume, David Punter:

- Establishes the classical background of metaphor from its philosophical roots to the religious and political tradition of metaphor in the East.
- Relates metaphor to the public realms of culture and politics and the way in which these influence the literary.
- Examines metaphor in relation to literary theory, philosophy, psychoanalysis and postcolonial studies.
- Illustrates his argument with specific examples from Western and Eastern literature and poetry.

This comprehensive and engaging book emphasises the significance of metaphor to literary studies, as well as its relevance to cultural studies, linguistics and philosophy.

David Punter is Professor of English Literature at the University of Bristol. He has published widely on Gothic, romantic and contemporary literature, psychoanalysis, postcolonial studies and literary theory.

THE NEW CRITICAL IDIOM

SERIES EDITOR: JOHN DRAKAKIS, UNIVERSITY OF STIRLING

The New Critical Idiom is an invaluable series of introductory guides to today's critical terminology. Each book:

- provides a handy, explanatory guide to the use (and abuse) of the term
- offers an original and distinctive overview by a leading literary and cultural critic
- relates the term to the larger field of cultural representation

With a strong emphasis on clarity, lively debate and the widest possible breadth of examples, *The New Critical Idiom* is an indispensable approach to key topics in literary studies.

Also available in this series:

METAPHOR

David Punter

Routledge
Taylor & Francis Group

LONDON AND NEW YORK

First published 2007 by Routledge
2 Park Square, Milton Park, Abingdon, Oxon OX14 4RN

Simultaneously published in the USA and Canada
by Routledge
270 Madison Ave, New York, NY 10016

Routledge is an imprint of the Taylor & Francis Group, an informa business

Typeset in Garamond and Scala Sans
by Keystroke, 28 High Street, Tettenhall, Wolverhampton
Printed and bound in Great Britain by
The Cromwell Press, Trowbridge, Wiltshire

British Library Cataloguing in Publication Data
A catalogue record for this book is available from the British Library

Library of Congress Cataloging in Publication Data
A catalog record for this book has been requested

ISBN13: 978–0–415–28165–2 (hbk)
ISBN13: 978–0–415–28166–9 (pbk)
ISBN13: 978–0–203–96588–7 (ebk)

CONTENTS

SERIES EDITOR'S PREFACE

The New Critical Idiom is a series of introductory books which seeks to extend the lexicon of literary terms, in order to address the radical changes which have taken place in the study of literature during the last decades of the twentieth century. The aim is to provide clear, well-illustrated accounts of the full range of terminology currently in use, and to evolve histories of its changing usage.

The current state of the discipline of literary studies is one where there is considerable debate concerning basic questions of terminology. This involves, among other things, the boundaries which distinguish the literary from the non-literary; the position of literature within the larger sphere of culture; the relationship between literatures of different cultures; and questions concerning the relation of literary to other cultural forms within the context of interdisciplinary studies.

It is clear that the field of literary criticism and theory is a dynamic and heterogeneous one. The present need is for individual volumes on terms which combine clarity of exposition with an adventurousness of perspective and a breadth of application. Each volume will contain as part of its apparatus some indication of the direction in which the definition of particular terms is likely to move, as well as expanding the disciplinary boundaries within which some of these terms have been traditionally contained. This will involve some re-situation of terms within the larger field of cultural representation, and will introduce examples from the area of film and the modern media in addition to examples from a variety of literary texts.

INTRODUCTION

We can begin to consider the study of metaphor by considering the nature of text, and of the word 'text' itself. If we were to be asked for a definition of 'text', our first recourse might be to a dictionary, and here we would find what at first glance appears to be precisely the definition we need:

> The wording of anything written or printed; the structure formed by the words in their order; the very words, phrases, and sentences as written.
>
> (*Oxford English Dictionary* [*OED*])

This may seem as though it is a clear, 'literal' meaning, and certainly it absolutely summarises some of the everyday uses of the word that we might make when contemplating the study of literature – although even here we may suspect that the dictionary meanings do not quite cover the expansion of the word 'text' into phrases like, for example, 'text-messaging'.

However, when we delve further into the dictionary definition, even this apparently solid ground starts to appear distinctly more unstable. Indeed, the further history of the word is supplied at the very head of the dictionary entry: it comes from the Latin verb 'texere', which means to weave. Thus, we might say, 'text' is something which is woven; but what exactly do we mean by this? Do we mean to refer to the original structure of paper, or papyrus, as something which was woven; or do we mean to refer to writing itself as something woven? Can we fully distinguish between the two? We may say that we have two images here, one of the paper, one of the words on the paper; but in the word 'text' these two images are brought together, and it would be difficult to say which of them has primacy.

Here, then, we are within a process of metaphor; a process, to use the most common definition of all, by means of which one thing is made to stand in for another thing. When we speak of 'twenty head of cattle' (which is a specific use of metaphor), we do not mean – and know that our hearers, or readers, will not expect us to mean – that twenty cows' heads are careering across the countryside, or indeed standing peaceably in a field; here the word 'head' does not have the customary meaning we might expect but rather stands in for another thing, for the cattle themselves. Specifically, this is an example of *metonymy*, the reduction of (in this case) the animal to a single representative element. And words, of course, especially common words like 'head', can have a multitude of meanings, often dependent on how and where they are used: the head of a school or other organisation, by which we mean the person in charge; the head of a river; the head by which we signify one side of a coin; the head of a weapon (such as we might find Geoffrey Chaucer alluding to in *The Tale of Sir Thopas* (1387) when he speaks of a spear being 'of fyn ciprees . . . The heed ful sharpe y-grounde' [Chaucer 1912: 504]); the head of a stringed musical instrument; the head of a bed; the head as the 'rounded leafy top of a tree or shrub', as the *OED* reminds us, giving an example of Edmund Spenser describing 'most dainty trees; that . . . seeme to bow their bloosming heads full lowe' (Spenser 2001: 702) – and so the list could go on. All these, we may say, are metaphorical usages, in that they adapt the root term 'head' as descriptive of a specific part of the body (human or otherwise) to other spheres of life; but as we look more closely, we may suspect that in fact the operations of metaphor go further than this. For all these usages rely, in one way or another, on the notion that the head is not merely the physically highest part of the human body; it is also, we have come to assume, the 'superior' part of the body in a less literal sense. It is true that this slippage can be justified by saying that we would not survive very long, or indeed at all, without a head; but neither would we last very long without a liver, or with no kidneys, yet we do not accord these organs the same status as the head.

What I mean to imply from this example, and to continue to explore in the following chapters, is that the processes of metaphor are everywhere at work in language. 'At work': and in using that term too I am venturing, inevitably, into the realm of the metaphorical. Of course, these processes are not sitting there, with a hammer and anvil, working away; when we say 'at work' we mean to suggest that something is happening, and that we need a suitable image in which to convey what it is that is happening. If all language is metaphorical, or at least invested with a certain metaphorical potential, then it could also follow that we might want to say that all language is continually involved in a series of acts of translation: translating things which are difficult to apprehend into things which we can apprehend, or conceptualise, or visualise, more easily. After all, all uses of language, from the very simplest to the most complex, are acts of communication, or at least they set out to be acts of communication whether they succeed or whether they fail, and therefore there is some implied motivation behind them, at some level, which seeks to engage the reader or listener. Metaphor seems to be integral to this need for engagement: even if we could conceive of a language without metaphor, which would be difficult to the point of impossibility, it would be a deeply drab and extremely restricted language. It could be, and has been, argued that such an imaginary language would approach the condition of mathematics, but even this seems doubtful; certainly the Roman numeral system is in a sense metaphorical, or at least 'figurative', in that the number of marks on the paper makes some attempt to represent figuratively the notions of one-ness, two-ness and so on.

One of the most frequent usages of metaphor is as *simile*. It has sometimes been supposed that simile is a different figure of speech from metaphor; but in fact it is a sub-species of metaphor, which is distinct only in that it keeps the notion of comparison explicit. In Graham Greene's *Brighton Rock* (1938), the anti-hero Pinkie experiences a moment when he almost repents of his many past villainies:

> He felt constriction and saw – hopelessly out of reach – a limitless freedom: no fear, no hatred, no envy. It was as if he were dead and were remembering the effect of a good confession, the words of absolution:

but being dead it was a memory only – he couldn't experience contrition – the ribs of his body were like steel bands which held him down to eternal unrepentance.

(Greene 1970: 179)

The simile here is expressed in 'like steel bands' (simile is always worded in terms of 'as' or 'like'): here Greene is comparing the spiritual constriction which afflicts Pinkie to a more physical, more conventionally material image, which both effects a specific connection with the reader and also expresses Pinkie's own need to translate his experience into something concrete.

Simile may be in one sense cruder than other forms of metaphor, in that it does not seek to conceal its artificiality; but alternatively one might say that it is the original form of metaphor. When camels are spoken of as 'ships of the desert', the missing word 'like' is, as it were, present but 'under erasure'; it has been omitted but the notion of 'likeness' continues.

As a different example of metaphor we might think about the word 'fascist'. Nowadays that word seems to have a field of precise connotations, largely held in political movements ('movements' is clearly another metaphor!) of the mid-twentieth century; but the word itself derives from another Latin term, the *fasces*, which were:

A bundle of rods bound up with an axe in the middle and its blade projecting. These rods were carried by lectors before the superior magistrates at Rome as an emblem of their power.

(*OED*)

We could fairly conjecture that when the fascist movement appropriated this image, this was done with an awareness of its metaphorical power; that what was being said, or indicated, was, for example, something about power and authority, and about the threat of violence at the heart of apparent order.

We do not necessarily think about, or even know of, these things now when we use the word 'fascist'; it would therefore be possible to suggest, as some critics and linguists have, that what we have here is a 'dead metaphor', in the sense of one where the original meanings and implications have been so eroded that they have become irrelevant to our processes of communication. But the question of when, or whether, a metaphor can ever be truly dead is a vexed one. Consider, for example, the first stanza of an apparently simple poem written by Philip Larkin, called 'How to Sleep' (1950):

> Child in the womb,
> Or saint on a tomb –
> Which way shall I lie
> To fall asleep?
> The keen moon stares
> From the back of the sky,
> The clouds are all home
> Like driven sheep.
>
> (Larkin 1988: 35)

Nobody, I think, would claim that the metaphors of a child in the womb and of a tomb effigy to represent sleep are new; indeed, they are so old that we barely perceive them as metaphorical at all. Indeed, when in a different poem, 'An Arundel Tomb' (1956), Larkin speaks of two such effigies on a tomb and says, 'They would not think to lie so long' (Larkin 1988: 110), the comparison between the stillness of the effigies and sleep is so quiet as to be barely perceptible. Similarly, the metaphor by means of which clouds become sheep is in no way new; on the contrary, it can be found in visual terms in hundreds of children's books.

Yet, it would be possible to contend that these apparently 'dead' metaphors are in fact revivified by their location in this stanza. Perhaps this is done by juxtaposition, because the image of the 'keen moon' staring 'from the back of the sky' is by no means moribund; the moon in Western tradition has a host of attributes (inconstant, deathly, pallid, but also, and sometimes contradictorily, regular, amorous, female) but 'keen' is not among them. This metaphor derives its force from the sense that the moon is not 'literally' 'keen' in either the sense of 'sharp and cutting' or 'enthusiastic or eager'. Indeed, the metaphor moves through the stanza, exercising a menacing force that might make us look again at the implicit violence of the image of the 'driven sheep'. In fact, by one of those complex tricks that language is constantly playing, the way 'keen' and 'moon' might really interact is by inviting us to see a picture of the moon 'keening' (a quite different word, meaning 'weeping' or 'mourning') over the scene, which in turn will colour in a mood and will induce us to doubt the apparent tranquillity of the child or the saint. This kind of phenomenon is very close to the force of the *homonym*, a term which refers to words which sound alike but have quite different meanings.

Let us briefly consider another metaphor. It occurs originally in a novel by Ian Fleming, *Dr No* (1958), but it has become the staple of the long series of James Bond films. We may note in passing that 'bond' is also a metaphor for the stability of the financial 'bond', and especially through a standard phrase, 'his word is his bond', it signifies honourableness or reliability. However, the particular phrases to which I want to call attention are: 'A medium Vodka dry Martini – with a slice of lemon peel. Shaken and not stirred' (Fleming 1958: 208). Almost every word of this quotation has metaphoric resonance. The word 'medium' signifies Bond's poise, his ability to remain centred while there is chaos around him. 'Dry' signifies a certain kind of 'dry wit', a wry amusement before the scenes of carnage which continually threaten to envelop him. The making of the martini with vodka – rather than, as more usually, with gin – signifies Bond's individuality, and simultaneously his calm and powerful ability to make the world accede to his wishes. The unusual precision of 'a slice of lemon peel' signifies his exactitude, his unwillingness to tolerate the second rate or second best.

As for 'shaken and not stirred', a whole litany of metaphorical equivalents could be read from this phrase. The contents are principally sexual and emotional: Bond as a character is perfectly willing to engage in sex (to be 'shaken'), but none of this will imply that he is 'stirred' (in its common metaphorical sense of being, or becoming, emotionally involved). In a broader sense, it implies Bond's willingness to become involved in the events around him without having the essence of his character changed. What is shaken returns eventually to its previous state; what is stirred might lose its pristine shape and become some kind of composite or compromise, but Bond's monosyllabic naming metaphorically signifies his essential separation from the world around him. And this spreads out to involve the reader, or the viewer of the films: we are expected to be 'shaken' by events, because otherwise we would not continue to follow the narrative in search of resolution; but in the end we are not expected to be stirred by them, because if we were we would be losing some of Bond's supposedly admirable *sang-froid* (a French term which could be translated as 'cold blood'). And so, from this brief comment, we find ourselves having metaphorical recourse to a whole myth of Englishness: calm amid surrounding pressures; resistant to the allurements of the foreign; capable of equipoise even under the most difficult of circumstances. Indeed, we might say that what Bond precisely does is to take elements of the foreign, such as vodka and martini, and 'translate' them into the props of an English myth.

In 1978, a conference on metaphor was held at the University of Chicago. One of the papers was by Wayne C. Booth, and it began as follows:

> There were no conferences on metaphor, ever, in any culture, until our own century was already middle-aged. As late as 1927, John Middleton Murry, complaining about the superficiality of most discussions of metaphor, could say, 'There are not many of them' . . . Explicit discussions of something called metaphor have multiplied astronomically in the past fifty years. This increase is not simply parallel to the vast increase in scholarly and critical writing. Shakespeareans have multiplied too, as have scholars of Homer, of Dickens, and of Charles the Second. But students of metaphor have positively pullulated . . . We shall soon no doubt have more metaphoricians than metaphysicians . . . I have in fact extrapolated with my pocket calculator to the year 2039; at that point there will be more students of metaphor than people.
>
> (Booth in Sacks 1979: 47)

Wayne Booth jests; nevertheless, and somewhat frighteningly, as I write we are almost up to the halfway point between 1978 and 2039, and the study of, and interest in, metaphor shows no signs of abating.

However, it is true that the study of metaphor has changed enormously over the last thirty years, and in ways which it would have been difficult to predict in 1978. The advent of new kinds of literary theory, the specific contributions of thinkers like Jacques Lacan and Jacques Derrida to the study of the text, the attention paid in new historicist and cultural materialist criticism to the formative power of tropes and rhetorics, all of these have in different ways contributed to revolutionising our thinking about metaphor. This book aims, then, to chart a path for the reader through these recent developments. Beginning by saying something about the classical background (Chapter 1), it then seeks to relativise this tradition by comparing it with Eastern versions of metaphor (Chapter 2), and to emphasise an essential continuity between ideas on metaphor and the public realms of language and politics (Chapter 3). Ways in which these public uses of metaphor influence the literary are examined in the chapter on the 'text instead' (Chapter 4). The insights of psychoanalysis are seen as essential to understanding the functioning of the metaphoric (Chapter 5), and metaphor is seen as being the very ground on which a text constantly goes beyond itself in an uncanny fashion, saying both more and less than it knows (Chapter 6). What remains important about metaphor, however, is to see it at all points as responsive to the wider cultural sphere, and especially as a site on which similarities and differences can be constructed and tested (Chapter 7); one of the crucial areas in which we can see metaphor functioning in literary and public ways, which the book will take as a specific example, is on the terrain of the postcolonial (Chapter 8). Although each of these chapters produces and looks at examples of metaphor from diverse fields, it is important to work through some examples in detail (Chapter 9), before moving to a conclusion which attempts to summarise for the reader recent developments and the current situation in the theory of metaphor (Chapter 10).

But before we 'embark' on this narrative, let us consider a final example of a metaphor which, while apparently simple, carries a remarkable freight of meanings and that also points to the crucial importance of metaphor in our daily lives. This concerns a firm of London builders from Indian backgrounds, who some years ago painted on the side of their van the slogan: 'You've tried the cowboys; now try the Indians'. In a way, metaphors of this kind, which are also jokes, or at the very least involved in a complex field of irony, are difficult to talk about, partly because talking about them threatens to unbalance the delicate poise that sustains the metaphor, especially as a kind of 'speech act'. However, we can at least do something to describe the metaphorical field at play here. We could begin with the usual meaning of the clichéd phrase 'cowboys and Indians' to describe a certain American cultural genre, chiefly represented in the movies but also present in the fictions of Zane Grey and others. And we could say that this is a metaphor in itself: it has come to stand in for a whole period of American history, with the concomitant idea that the white men who are signified by the 'cowboys' represent the 'side of good' against the primitive world of the North American Indian. This, however, is cross-cut with another myth, which is of the 'outlaw': the perpetuation of the myth, which is still very much with us today, if only in the 'survivalist' conditions of the extreme American rural right or in the Texan rhetoric of George W. Bush, clearly supports the metaphor of the cowboy as somebody who lives outside the law and yet has his own codes and practices of honour. As Bob Dylan encapsulated the myth, 'to live outside the law, you must be honest' (Dylan 1994: 349).

This is a metaphor which has now come to support a notion of US individualism. We are a long way from a 1787 usage of the term, 'A Flaxen headed cow boy, as simple as may be' (Bickerstaffe *et al.* 1792: II, 36), where the term is used in support of a non-violent pastoral myth. Instead, we have here the cultural transition to the common trope of the 'cowboy builder', which carries various metaphorical connotations: lawless, certainly, but in a distinctly unpleasant sense, as somebody who rides in by day and rides out again by night, leaving the job unfinished, the stairs waiting to fall down as soon as they are trodden on.

But our builders have picked up on another stream of metaphorical meanings, concerning, first, the stereotypical treatment of the 'Indians' in Western films; this stereotype is based on a cardinal misnomer, however, since the reason American Indians are called 'Indians' at all is a reflection of the colossal mistakes of Western explorers concerning what they thought they had found, and where they thought they were, when they lighted on the shores of America. Here there is a more or less forcible rejoining of this meaning of 'Indian' to the older idea of somebody who comes from the subcontinent of India. There is thus a certain deliberate 'inappropriateness' to this metaphor; it is not designed to suggest or produce an exact 'fit' between two different ideas or images; rather, it is supposed to challenge the reader to look at the fissures, the cracks in our cultural conception of the 'Indian'.

And this, I suggest, we shall find whenever we look closely at metaphor; although metaphor undoubtedly deals in likeness, similarity, it also deals in unlikeness and dissimilarity. Metaphor makes us look at the world afresh, but it often does so by challenging our notions of the similarity that exists between things; how alike they are; and in what ways, in fact, they are irreconcilably unalike. Thus, metaphor represents a basic operation of language: it seeks to 'fix' our understanding, but at the same time it reveals how any such fixity, any such desire for stability and certainty, is constructed on shifting sands.

'Shifting sands', to conclude, is obviously a metaphor; here, I hope, it is one that is being used accurately in order to provide an image of dangerous uncertainty, and indeed the threat of engulfment. If we think of another 'sand' metaphor, 'to draw a line in the sand', it is remarkable how this metaphor has come, certainly in recent years, and perhaps especially in the hands of politicians, to reverse its own signification. 'To draw a line in the sand' is clearly an impossible, or at best a somewhat temporary, task; but when politicians seek to convince a sceptical public that they are about to seal off some dreadful past event or strategic failure, this seems to be the metaphor towards which they reach, unaware (we hope) that the metaphor is itself constantly undermining their claims to be in control of circumstances.

1

THE CLASSICAL PROBLEM
FIGURATIVE LANGUAGE

Let us now turn to the history of metaphor. Since at least the time of Aristotle, it would appear that Western literary, linguistic and critical traditions have been interested in the possibility of differentiating between literal and figurative language. Within that general process, attention has focused on establishing a system both on which to base this differentiation and within which to distinguish further between different types of the figurative. Within these extensive and complex traditions, it is possible to establish a continuing dialogue between different valuations of the figurative, and consequently between, on the one hand, views of metaphor as adornment or elaboration, and, on the other, metaphor as the basic structure of language, according to which representations offer 'versions' of referents and thus inevitably imply an 'originary' process of metaphorisation.

There is no better place to begin than with Aristotle, who is generally regarded as the first thinker to elaborate a theory of metaphor. In his *Poetics* (350 BC), Aristotle first characterises it as a sign of absolute linguistic mastery and, therefore, of a certain type of genius. As he says, 'It is the one thing that cannot be learnt from others, and it is also a sign of genius, since a good metaphor implies an intuitive perception of the similarity in dissimilars' (Aristotle 1909: 71). Far more important, though, is that Aristotle located the specific use of metaphor in poetry rather than in either of the other great divisions of discourse: rhetoric and logic. By doing so, he makes it clear that he does not regard metaphor as integral to language's functioning; rather, it is a kind of decoration or ornament. It has the power to please, which is an exciting and perhaps, under some circumstances, a dangerous power; but it is in some sense an addition to the 'normal', by which we might infer 'literal', workings of language. Aristotle further defines metaphor as 'giving the thing a name that belongs to something else; the transference being either from genus to species, or from species to genus, or from species to species, or on grounds of analogy' (Aristotle 1909: 63). Behind this there lies the notion that every 'thing' in nature has its own 'proper name'; metaphor constitutes a kind of infringement of this rule, whereby 'names' are conveyed from one thing to another. This may be done, as we have seen earlier, in the literal comparisons of simile; or there may be a certain 'hidden-ness' which is more typical of other processes of metaphor. At all events, the underlying intent, according to Aristotle, is to point out resemblances; these resemblances may move the reader or hearer beyond the 'usual' linguistic and rhetorical rules of clarity and decorum, but they are justified because the reader is, as it were, 'brought up short'; he or she is in the presence of something unusual, something outside language's normal ambit, and this can serve to deepen the reader's experience, to bring a suddenly enriched apprehension of the world.

The actress Vivien Leigh once said of the dramatist and political thinker George Bernard Shaw: 'Shaw is like a train. One just speaks the words and sits in one's place. But Shakespeare is like bathing in the sea – one swims where one wants' (quoted in Nicolson 1968: 297). Now this is what we might well recognise as the simplest form of metaphor – simile, where the comparison, the 'transference' (*metapherein*) between the two entities, is explicitly signalled by the word 'like' (or sometimes 'as'). Some would say that this is the basic form of all metaphor; what causes metaphors which are not cast in the linguistic form of the simile to have greater power is precisely the omission of the 'like', an omission which brings the two compared entities far closer to each other in a way that challenges the reader or hearer to make sense of the assumed or alleged comparison rather than having it spelt out. The point here, however, is that the reader is expected to gain some additional understanding from the analogies presented. George Bernard Shaw is not, in fact, very much like a train; he was smaller, for a start, and had no engine. However, there is sufficient similarity for the reader to pause, to have the opportunity to recognise a new connection; to, as Aristotle put it, 'get hold of something fresh'. The parallels here are to do with running tracks, with a certain lack of freedom, with inducing a certain passivity in the watcher, here equated with a passenger. William Shakespeare is, perhaps, also not much like the sea, although the array of metaphors which have been deployed to explain his pre-eminent position in drama and in the English national culture suggest an unceasing quest to find metaphors apt to convey the complexity, the freedom, the spacious- ness of Shakespeare's drama. Ben Jonson, for example, referred to him as 'Sweet swan of Avon' (Jonson 1975: 265); Samuel Johnson compared Corneille to Shakespeare 'as a clipped hedge is to a forest' (quoted in Piozzi 1925: 41); John Dryden referred to Shakespeare as the 'very Janus of poets; he wears almost everywhere two faces; and you have scarce begun to admire the one, ere you despise the other' (Dryden 1926: I, 172); Samuel Taylor Coleridge referred to him as 'myriad-minded' (Coleridge 1956: 175), and also said that 'the body and substance of his works came out of the unfathomable depths of his own oceanic mind' (Coleridge 1990: I, 468).

What this might suggest is that metaphor – and I am going to continue to suggest that 'metaphorisation', although perhaps a little clumsy, would be a better word – is not so much an occasional intrusion into 'normal' patterns of speech; rather, it constitutes a continuing process of 'translation'. Where a concept, an idea, an emotion may be hard to grasp in language, then a metaphor, an offering of perceived resemblances, may enable us the better to 'come to grips with' the issue in hand. To follow Shakespeare obliquely through another twist, in 1941 we find George Orwell searching for adequate metaphors to describe the contemporary state of England:

> England is not the jewelled isle of Shakespeare's much-quoted passage, nor is it the inferno described by Dr Goebbels. More than either it resembles a family, a rather stuffy Victorian family, with not many black sheep in it but with all its cupboards bursting with skeletons . . . A family with the wrong members in control.
>
> (Orwell 1941: 35)

This passage can helpfully introduce us to two further features of metaphor. First, it is clear that here Orwell has a political intent: he means to divorce the imagery of England from, on the one hand, the smug over-optimism with which Shakespeare's original image, whatever *its* intent, could be interpreted for a modern world; and probably more importantly, he wishes to divorce it, in time of war, from the antagonistic characterisation mounted by Goebbels, the Nazi propagandist, which itself, in the mind of Orwell or Goebbels, probably takes us back to Dante's description of hell in his *Inferno* (early fourteenth century). Metaphor, in other words, is rarely if ever innocent; it has designs on us, as Aristotle and the other Greek philosophers of language indeed recognised. Second, Orwell's comment reveals the way in which the complexity of metaphor often entails metaphors nesting, as it were, inside one another; the black sheep and the skeletons in the cupboard are themselves metaphors which Orwell brings to bear to sustain his 'master-metaphor' of the Victorian family as an image of the condition of England.

Already we are up against questions about metaphor as mere 'ornamentation'; to sustain such an argument would imply that Shakespeare's admirers and critics, or Orwell, could in some sense have 'made their point' in some other, more 'literal' way. But this is, to say the least, highly arguable. To move to a radically different field: when the Conservative Party came up in 1978 with the election slogan 'Labour isn't working', the intention was to juxtapose two different ideas. The first, reinforced by the accompanying picture of a queue outside an unemployment office, was that under a Labour government unemployment was rife; the second was to imply that the Labour government was 'not working' in the sense that it was being ineffectual. But it is not easy to see how this slogan could have been expressed in any other form; certainly had such an attempt been made it would have been inordinately long and, perhaps more to the point, inordinately boring. Also, by spelling out the connection between the hidden statements, there would have been the danger of a certain subterfuge being exposed, of voters wondering whether the system of cause and effect proposed in the slogan really withstood closer scrutiny.

There is here a whole set of questions about *latent* and *manifest* meaning. The metaphor can be considered in some sense and under some circumstances to be a kind of sleight of hand by means of which meanings can be surreptitiously smuggled into an apparently innocent discourse. In this context, classical definitions of metaphor have tended to try to separate the material of the metaphor into two levels: the 'tenor', or the material which is supposed to be conveyed by the metaphor; and the 'vehicle', which is the term for the image doing the conveying. But in this particular slogan it is difficult, if not impossible, to provide such a hierarchical arrangement; the intention is to convey both ideas simultaneously, and to solder them together in the mind of the recipient. The use of metaphor, we might say, in the hands of politicians is nothing less than an attempt to rewire the brain, if only on a temporary basis; that this is also true of advertisers is perhaps too obvious to mention, although it is worth saying that Judith Williamson's pioneering *Decoding Advertisements* (1978) remains a crucial book to read in this connection.

The view of metaphor not as ornamentation but as integral to language emerges at various points in Western literary history, but perhaps most decisively with the romantic poets of the late eighteenth and early nineteenth centuries. Coleridge, for example, refers to what he calls the 'two cardinal points of poetry' as the following: 'the power of exciting the sympathy of the reader by a faithful adherence to the truth of nature, and the power of giving the interest of novelty by the modifying colours of the imagination' (Coleridge 1956: 168). These two skills, or faculties, cannot be separated; they are integrally joined in a particular use of language. And for Coleridge, as well as for other romantics, this use of language was as essential to criticism as it was to poetry or any other type of writing. Consider, for example, his remarkable comment on the prose style of the great historian Edward Gibbon:

> When I read a chapter in Gibbon I seem to be looking through a luminous haze or fog, figures come and go, I know not how or why, all larger than life or distorted or discoloured; nothing is real, vivid, true; all is scenical, and by candle light as it were.
>
> (Coleridge 1990: I, 418–19)

This extraordinary description is clearly metaphorical. We do not suppose that when Coleridge read Gibbon he felt himself to be literally enveloped in a luminous haze, but we do suppose that in the very attempt to convey with the utmost clarity to his own readers his feelings when he read Gibbon he ineluctably found himself searching for a metaphor which would be not only the most apt but, precisely and using his own terms, the most *vivid* way of communicating his own experience. This is a paradoxical clarity since what Coleridge is attempting to convey here is a kind of essence of unclarity.

Elsewhere in Coleridge's writing this use of metaphor is evident. Let us consider the opening to one of his best-known poems, 'Kubla Khan' (1798):

> In Xanadu did Kubla Khan
> A stately pleasure dome decree:
> Where Alph, the sacred river, ran
> Through caverns measureless to man
>   Down to a sunless sea.
> So twice five miles of fertile ground
> With walls and towers were girdled round:
> And there were gardens bright with sinuous rills,
> Where blossomed many an incense-bearing tree;
> And here were forests ancient as the hills,
> Enfolding sunny spots of greenery.
>
> (Coleridge 1967: 297)

It appears obvious from the very first line of this poem that we are here in the presence of a metaphorical structure; we do not suppose that this 'pleasure dome' is, or was, in some sense literal, partly because, were it indeed to be merely so, it would be difficult to see how it could interest us one way or the other as to whether a long-dead Mongol emperor happened to indulge his passion and wealth in such an architectural construction. We might instead view the beginning of this poem as what we might call an 'invitation to metaphorisation'; in other words, we *expect*, as perhaps we do with most poems, and often with other works of literature as well, there to be a metaphorical dimension, in this case to discover that this 'pleasure-dome' stands in for something else.

Coleridge famously claimed to have been interrupted in the writing of 'Kubla Khan' by the arrival of the infamous 'person on business from Porlock' (Coleridge 1967: 296), and so it has always been difficult to know whether the poem is in any sense a 'whole'. And yet, as we contemplate it in the form available to us, we need also to acknowledge that that process of metaphorisation is not closed; we may feel ourselves here to be in the presence of metaphor, but precisely what that metaphor *is* may well remain opaque. A metaphor then, we might reasonably surmise, is not necessarily a matter of simple one-to-one equivalents ('this stands in for that'), but neither is it a process of ornamentation of something that could have been more clearly said in another, simpler way; rather, in this case at least, as in the very different case of the party political slogan quoted above, it *is* the very substance of the discourse. A common error about metaphor is to suppose that it can be in some sense 'unpacked'. When that unpacking takes place, what is left is rarely of value; it seems a paltry and colourless thing when compared with the metaphor itself.

In some ways this connects metaphor to the language of dream, and this is a connection we shall explore later; suffice here to say that it is obviously no accident that Coleridge subtitled 'Kubla Khan' 'A Vision in a Dream'. It also places under scrutiny, as many philosophers of language from Max Black onwards have done, the whole question of *meaning* in relation to metaphor. Does a metaphor *mean* something more than, or different from, or in some sense beneath, what it appears to say; or is the meaning of a metaphor precisely what it *does* say? Joseph Conrad has a pertinent comment related to this issue in *Heart of Darkness* (1902), at the moment when the narrator is trying to describe Marlow's manner of telling a story:

> The yarns of seamen have a direct simplicity, the whole meaning of which lies within the shell of a cracked nut. But Marlow was not typical (if his propensity to spin yarns be excepted), and to him the meaning of an episode was not inside like a kernel but outside, enveloping the tale which brought it out only as a glow brings out a haze, in the likeness of one of these misty halos that sometimes are made visible by the spectral illumination of moonshine.
>
> (Conrad 1983: 30)

This, I suggest, might itself be a useful metaphor for the concept of metaphor; that it may not be revealed by an 'opening' or unpacking, but rather that it gives off its own meaning in a way that is difficult of apprehension but integral to communication and understanding. It is perhaps also worth bearing in mind that, later, Marlow himself refers to the attempt to render events into language in Coleridgean, or even Freudian, terms as indistinguishable from dream. 'Do you see the story?' he asks. 'Do you see anything?'

> It seems to me I am trying to tell you a dream – making a vain attempt, because no relation of a dream can convey the dream-sensation, that commingling of absurdity, surprise, and bewilderment in a tremor of struggling revolt, that notion of being captured by the incredible which is of the very essence of dreams.
>
> (Conrad 1983: 57)

And then, a little later, he adds, in a famous line, 'We live, as we dream – alone'.

It may seem as though we have moved a little way from metaphor here, but the point I am making is that as the view of language as predominantly metaphorical has gained ground, then this may be seen as an accompaniment to a re-examination of the whole question of the possibility of discourse delivering verifiable truths. This has come continuingly under question recently, not only in literature but also in the physical sciences, and what Conrad is here presciently recognising is that if all language is fundamentally metaphorical, then the meanings it enshrines cannot be re-expressed in any other way; they cannot be made clearer by some attempt to expunge metaphor from the linguistic register.

We might also wish to say that the critical discussion of metaphor has, since the romantic literary revolution, necessarily to an extent proceeded in the light of changes in literary, and perhaps especially poetic, practice. When we read, for example, a passage from the Augustan poet Alexander Pope it is not difficult to apprehend the concept of metaphor as ornamentation. There is a famously vitriolic episode in the *Epistle to Dr Arbuthnot* (1734) where Pope attacks the character whom he chooses to name Sporus:

> Let Sporus tremble – 'What? that thing of silk,
> Sporus, that mere white curd of Ass's milk?
> Satire or sense, alas! can Sporus feel?
> Who breaks a butterfly upon a wheel?'
>   Yet let me flap this bug with gilded wings,

This painted child of dirt, that stinks and stings;
Whose buzz the witty and the fair annoys,
Yet wit ne'er tastes, and beauty ne'er enjoys:
So well-bred spaniels civilly delight
In mumbling of the game they dare not bite.
Eternal smiles his emptiness betray,
As shallow streams run dimpling all the way.
Whether in florid impotence he speaks,
And, as the prompter breathes, the puppet squeaks;
Or at the ear of Eve, familiar Toad,
Half froth, half venom, spits himself abroad,
In puns, or politics, or tales, or lies,
Or spite, or smut, or rhymes, or blasphemies.
His wit all see-saw, between *that* and *this*,
Now high, now low, now Master up, now Miss,
And he himself one vile Antithesis.

(Pope 1966: 336–7)

Here we have a poetic method which deliberately and indeed ostentatiously displays the poet's control of metaphor; indeed, we notice that the poet's self-differentiation from Sporus is partly based on this factor. The wit of Pope's metaphors is precisely an *enactment* of his assumed literary, moral and characterological superiority over the unfortunate Sporus. And we notice too that in order to achieve this effect Pope does not reside within a single structure of equivalence. He compares Sporus first to a 'thing of silk' (tremulous and inconstant, but also anticipating through the figure of the silk-worm the later insect analogies); then to the 'curd of Ass's milk', with its connotations of something that has curdled – the metaphor 'white' here has been wrenched from its more usual connotations of purity and made instead to represent something pallid and sickly; then to a 'butterfly', something which has no weight, no solidity, something which we might say is, indeed, paradoxically unworthy of the very weight of metaphor which Pope is bringing to bear upon his subject.

The butterfly – which, after all, has residual metaphorical connotations of beauty and a wondrous fragility – is then transmuted into a 'bug' that 'stinks and stings'; by now this insect, whatever it is, is being regarded as simply a nuisance, a frivolous but damaging excrescence on society. But then again Pope changes his ground, to the image of the spaniel, not here being considered for its connotations of faithfulness and love, but rather for its 'fawning' quality. Next we come to the 'dimpling' stream, with its connotations of inconstancy and, more particularly, of a fair appearance which barely masks a worthless shallowness. It is worth remarking here that Pope is quite consciously reversing the very different metaphorical force which a 'dimpling stream' might have in a different kind of poem, of beauty and naturalness. We then move, again continuing the stream of animal metaphors, to the 'Toad', who, through the association with Eve, here clearly stands in for the Devil, yet even here the image of the toad is still further undermined as we are supposed to hear that the tempting voice he uses is not even his own but rather that of a puppet being manipulated by some greater force. The image by now constructed is therefore of somebody who is in no sense 'master' of himself, but rather of somebody who fawns upon other masters. Indeed, this is taken still further in the last lines of the extract, where the so far partly hidden accusations of gender uncertainty become explicit ('now Master up, now Miss'), and Pope more or less directly accuses Sporus of a sexual ambivalence which, in terms of the metaphorical structure of the passage, underlines his moral worthlessness.

Pope here is not ashamed of 'decoration'; on the contrary, he is contemptuously demonstrating that his gift for the ornament is far superior to that of Sporus. The animal metaphors serve, all too viciously, their purpose; but in asserting similarity Pope is not meaning us in any sense to mistake one thing for another. On the contrary, he is seeking to encourage the reader to share his denigration of Sporus, and to have that reinforced by the poet's own mastery, his own linguistic and metaphorical skill.

When we place a pre-romantic poem like Pope's against a very different poem from the twentieth century, immediately we see how impossible it would be to paraphrase or describe this poem in terms of metaphor as ornamentation. Following the theme of animal metaphors, we might look at George MacBeth's remarkable poem 'Owl' (1963), of which the first three stanzas or so run as follows:

Owl

is my favourite. Who flies
like a nothing through the night,

who-whoing. Is a feather
duster in leafy corners ring-a-rosying
boles of mice. Twice

you hear him call. Who
is he looking for? You hear
him hoovering over the floor
of the wood. O would you be gold
rings in the driving skull

if you could? Hooded and
vulnerable by the winter suns
owl looks. Is the grain of bark
in the dark. Round beaks are at
work in the pellety nest,

resting.

(MacBeth 1964: 117)

There are many things one could say about this poem; one could talk about its rhyme scheme, and especially the remarkable use of internal rhyme. One could talk about the syntactical distortions (later phrases include 'Is a goad', 'Am an owl'). But here our concern is metaphor, and it is particularly interesting to see how this poem demonstrates a significant possibility for metaphor, namely that, at least as taken in one direction, it tends towards a certain kind of what we might reasonably call 'incarnation'. In a note to the poem, MacBeth writes: 'Someone, perhaps a child, who is fascinated by owls creates a sort of spell to bring an owl into being. By the end of the poem he has become the owl' (MacBeth 1964: 121).

We do not have to accept this view of the poem; authors' remarks on their own works do not constitute explanations, although they may very well constitute, in cases such as this, valuable addenda to the works in question. The point at stake here, in the poem and in MacBeth's comment on it, is rather to do with the way in which the key metaphor of the poem 'brings something into being'. For Pope and his contemporaries, such a contention would have seemed nonsensical: poems do not bring things into being; rather, they are exercises of wit, demonstrations of linguistic skill. If you had been foolish enough to ask Pope, 'Well, is Sporus *actually* a butterfly?', he would no doubt, and with good reason, have thought you mad.

The case here is not so simple. If you removed the metaphors from the Pope passage, you could still construct a searing indictment of Sporus from the suggestions that the metaphors encourage. To remove the owl from the MacBeth poem would be impossible, unthinkable; the relation between the metaphor and any 'literal' truth which it may be assumed to mask or code is far more condensed, even fused. The owl does not, for example, act as a substitute for any specific human qualities, any more than the human can be seen to stand in for the owl; rather, two dissimilars are brought together and 'yoked' (to use Samuel Johnson's rather disparaging word in the rather different context of metaphysical poetry) together.

In the service of this major metaphor, or indeed 'conceit' as the metaphysical poets would have called it, many 'minor metaphors' are brought into play. There is the notion of the owl as a 'nothing', bringing out his silence and, certainly from the point of view of his prey, invisibility. There is the comparison to a 'feather duster', which works both through the impression of an indistinct bundle of feathers and also through the less obvious attribution to the owl of a certain harmlessness, which is presumably how his victims are meant to see him until it is too late. There is the image of the children's game of 'Ring-a-Ring-a-Roses'; as readers we may or may not know that the origins of this game lie in the years of the Great Plague, but even if we do not we will still find something sinister in this metaphorical juxtaposition of the apparent innocence of a children's game with the violence of the owl's dealings with the world.

And this is only in the first stanza. The correlation is not merely between the human and the owl; rather, the metaphorical structure is extended as the owl becomes increasingly assimilated to a kind of 'spirit of place'. 'Is the grain of bark/in the dark': the surface implication is again about the owl's invisibility and his capacity for camouflage, about his ability to be unseen by those whom he is about to seize; but the metaphor also gives us a sense of the owl being an inalienable part of the world he inhabits. The owl works, we might say, within rather than against the grain; the implication is that he is perfectly designed, perfectly suited, to the life he leads, in a way which human beings, who have choices of a kind which an owl cannot experience, will never be.

Within the metaphor, then, there is thus also a certain kind of envy, a sense given of a different kind of life which is both rougher and more simple. 'O would you be gold/rings in the driving skull/if you could?': the force of this metaphor of the 'gold rings' is, at one level, to remind us of the physical shape of the owl's face, his eyes, but also to invoke a metaphor of value, of force. At the same time it also reminds us that the owl, as he appears to his victims, may indeed appear only to be a pair of 'gold rings', only the feathers around the eyes visible in that final moment of panic and death.

'Owl', then, represents a kind of metaphor which cannot be properly separated into 'vehicle' and 'tenor'. Rather, it reveals something of the metaphorical ground on which, by means of notions of similarity and difference, we construct our notions of what it is to be human, and also, by implication, of what it is that we conceal, repress, but continue to feel attracted to in the 'not human', in the creature of drives which, we might think after Freud, continues to inhabit us all.

A structure of metaphor which is both similar and different can be found in the American writer Cormac McCarthy's novel *The Crossing* (1993). Here we are partly inside the mind of a hungry, cold, lost wolf:

> She wandered the eastern slopes of the Sierra de la Madera for a week. Her ancestors had hunted camels and primitive toy horses on these grounds. She found little to eat. Most of the game was slaughtered out of the country. Most of the forest cut to feed the boilers of the stamp-mills at the mines. The wolves in that country had been killing cattle for a long time but the ignorance of the animals was a puzzle to them. The cows bellowing and bleeding and stumbling through the mountain meadows with their shovel feet and their confusion, bawling and floundering through the fences and dragging posts and wires behind. The ranchers said they brutalized the cattle in a way they did not the wild game. As if the cows evoked in them some anger. As if they were offended by some violation of an old order. Old ceremonies. Old protocols.

> (McCarthy 2002: 331)

The metaphorical structure of this passage, especially as considered in terms of relations between the categories of the human and the animal, works in a number of different ways. Most obviously, what we have here is a sustained metaphor, in the figures of the wolves and the ranchers, for the relation between the wild and the tame. But within this structure, many things shift place. For example, the wolves are here credited with something akin to human memory, some inner longevity which quite belies their being as beasts of immediate, spontaneous impulse; thus, it is the wolves which are made to carry the history, indeed the prehistory, of the 'country', whatever country this is, while the ranchers are regarded as *parvenus* who know or remember nothing of the 'old order'.

Between these two poles of the metaphor, the cattle stumble and flounder. The implication clearly is that the wolves remember some older, more primitive form of hunting, where the prey had their own methods of evasion, their own competencies, because, precisely, they had themselves not been tamed. But these cattle, these tame beasts, the wolves cannot understand at all; they no longer belong in the domain of the wild – they have been weirdly transferred to the other side of the metaphorical structure, to the territory of man; which means, in turn, that they have lost the status of the beast – they no longer know where they are or where they have been.

The notion of 'anger' in this passage could hardly function without some notion of metaphor, or indeed without some kind of anthropomorphism or a concept of the 'transferred epithet', which begins to reveal something of one of the psychological roots of metaphor, which we will develop later. For the notion that 'some old anger' is evoked in the wolves by the site of domestication is quite obviously here a kind of metaphorical reversal of the ranchers' feelings about the wolves themselves, feelings which become clearer in other passages in the book. Indeed, the whole notion of attributing to animals such negative attributes as 'savagery', 'bestiality', the commonplace but ludicrous simile 'he behaved like an animal', as though it were possible for an animal to behave in a 'depraved' way, can be read as a projection not of animal behaviour but rather of human fears. These fears would not only be reflections of our primitive fear of animals, and especially of predatory animals, themselves; it would also be a fear, commonplace throughout human history but perhaps especially noticeable, in Britain at least, in the wake of Darwinian discoveries, of an eruption of the beast inside the human self, of being forced to own to, or perhaps quail before, something within the category of the human which is distinctly *not* human. We may be reminded of this by our own warlike excesses or by our condemnatory attitudes to ordinary animal behaviour. This passage points one stage beyond that: in the world which the wolf is encountering, no 'naturalness' of any kind remains; all has been changed by what we might loosely term a 'human imperialist exploitation'. What has transformed the cattle will, in the end, also transform the wolf; or, if it does not, then the wolf will disappear, in terms not only of evolution but of narrative, because it will no longer have any part to play in the anthropomorphic unfolding of human drama.

2

EASTERN AND
WESTERN METAPHOR

Western notions of metaphor, therefore, depend on specific registers of similarity and dissimilarity, but metaphor has occupied a quite different place in the long evolution of Eastern critical theories, and this is in part a consequence of the different emphases and valuations placed upon writing and speech. Thus, in order to pursue a history of metaphor, it is necessary to turn aside and look at the role of metaphor in the establishment of Chinese and Japanese poetics. Here the relation between text and physicality takes a different turn, as does the relation between consciousness and the unconscious, and consequently the role of metaphor as mediation between self and 'not-self'. Metaphor in the Chinese tradition, for example, is bound to a theory of 'appropriate styles'; but what is also important is that it is responsive to a quite different religious and political tradition, and thus these differences can be used to demonstrate the necessary instability of general definitions of metaphor, as I shall go on to show.

I have already mentioned various terms which are loosely associated with metaphor, and now is a moment to try to be clear about these terms as they have traditionally been used within the Western tradition. The term 'metaphor' itself is seen to identify a verbal process whereby two discrete objects or ideas become linked, but in a very particular way, such that, for the duration of the metaphor, one of the items actually becomes the other, and vice versa: if we say, 'James is a beast', we are not merely inviting our listener to adjudicate on exactly in what way James displays any one or more of a range of beast-like qualities; rather, we are inviting the listener to identify James with a beast.

A simile, as we have seen, proposes a looser form of association. If we say, 'James behaves like a spaniel', we are inviting the listener to consider the way or ways in which James resembles a spaniel and, perhaps, even to adjudicate for him- or herself as to whether the comparison is apt. But similes depend, like all forms of metaphor, on a certain degree of common ground. If we were instead to have said, 'James is like an armadillo', we could reasonably expect considerably more puzzlement on the part of listeners as they try to work out in what way or ways James resembles an armadillo, which might be somewhat more testing in terms of our knowledge of, or assumptions about, natural history.

It is also conventional to isolate as a separate category what is often referred to as an 'extended metaphor'. Here a metaphor might extend itself beyond a single point of comparison and run through an entire passage of text, or an entire poem, as it did in the MacBeth poem quoted in Chapter 1. Perhaps the greatest master of the extended metaphor is Charles Dickens. The following example is a passage from *The Mystery of Edwin Drood* (1870), introducing a chapter called 'A Dean, and a Chapter Also':

> Whosoever has observed that sedate and clerical bird, the rook, may perhaps have noticed that when he wings his way homeward towards nightfall, in a sedate and clerical company, two rooks will suddenly detach themselves from the rest, will retrace their flight for some distance, and will there poise and linger; conveying to mere men the fancy that it is of some occult importance to the body politic, that this artful couple should pretend to have renounced connection with it.
>
> Similarly, service being over in the old Cathedral with the square tower, and the choir scuffling out again, and divers venerable persons of rook-like aspect dispersing, two of these latter retrace their steps, and walk together in the echoing Close.
>
> (Dickens 1974: 40)

Dickens sets the scene by an extended comparison between clergymen and rooks, in the course of which the similarities are drawn out in order to engage the attention and imagination. Sometimes he even develops a method whereby the name of a character, such as Mrs Gamp, for example, or Biler, continues throughout the particular novel to carry these metaphorical significations. Indeed, in certain cases, such as that of Mr Micawber, these associations, this 'continuous' process of metaphorisation, have entered into the culture in such a way that the name itself cannot be mentioned without drawing in its wake a chain of metaphorical associations.

The end-point, one might say, of these extended metaphorical processes is allegory. Here we would be talking about a text which assumes a readerly understanding that whenever a character or event is mentioned, it stands in for another character or event. Sometimes allegory is regarded as a particularly crude form of metaphor, in the sense that it invites the reader to do little work. Instead, it invites them into a pre-established framework of correspondences; cardinal cases of this process might include novels of anti-totalitarian satire such as Aldous Huxley's *Brave New World* (1932) and George Orwell's *1984* (1948). In other cases, such as Spenser's *The Faerie Queene* (1590–96), the allegory can be extremely subtle and rely on readerly understandings of a very complex kind. The most obvious example in the history of allegory, John Bunyan's *The Pilgrim's Progress* (1676), achieves its effect not by asking the reader to form new connections but by inviting them into an existing network of metaphors: the names of Bunyan's characters – such as Christian and Faithful – mean exactly what they say, and there is little room for character subtlety or manoeuvre in their interpretation. If, however, we take a case which is in some way dependent on Bunyan but written much later, Wilkie Collins's *The Woman in White* (1860), where the protagonist is known as 'Hartright', we are in a more complex field: the name 'Hartright' may well suggest, in a Bunyanesque way, a hero of perfect moral rectitude, but in *The Woman in White* Collins is inviting us to inspect whether this is indeed an accurate epithet for his protagonist, or whether, as seems more likely, he is in fact somewhat blinded by his own rectitude as to what is going on around him.

Synecdoche is another term for a figure of speech which some would take to be a variant of metaphor, whereby part of an object is taken to stand in for the whole, as in 'sail' for ships or, as we have seen, 'head' for cattle; and there have, over the years, been many other terms devised for specific and detailed figures of speech, or tropes, which can be seen to be sub-categories of metaphor. Many metaphors are anthropomorphic, which means that the type of comparison they seek makes something non-human into something human. This may be something inanimate, and the constant reference to ships as 'she' is a case in point. Or it may be a non-human animal, as in the ways in which pets of various descriptions are endowed, sometimes to a bizarre extent, with quasi-human attributes. Indeed, it may be said that the whole kind of relationship suggested by the notion of the pet, which is quite culturally and historically specific, and not to be found in many cultures, is intrinsically metaphorical in that it seeks to replace the animality of the animal with a substituted human sensibility and with apparently human behaviours.

The term 'extended metaphor' can itself be further extended. To take one example: as is well known, there emerged in the late eighteenth century in Britain and Europe, and subsequently in America, a subgenre of fiction called 'Gothic'. When we think of Gothic, one thing that certainly comes to mind is the specific and limited range of metaphors with which the early texts played. For example, the list of Gothic works containing the word 'castle' in their title, let alone using the castle as the major setting for the action, is enormous, from Horace Walpole's *The Castle of Otranto* (1765), supposedly the originator of the genre, through Ann Radcliffe's *The Castles of Athlin and Dunbayne* (1789) and beyond. Although the word 'castle' does not appear in the title, Mervyn Peake's *Gormenghast* trilogy (1946–59) may well be regarded as a late avatar of the genre.

That the castle is some kind of metaphor would seem clear: after all, the contemporary reader's interest in castles as such is presumably limited. But for what is it a metaphor? Critics have suggested many options. The castle can be seen as a place of absolute political power, of a kind which is both hated and envied in the more volatile situation of late eighteenth- and early nineteenth-century Europe. It can be seen in psychological terms as a place of enclosure, a womb-like edifice which is, again, both feared and longed for, as a place of confinement and/or as a place of safety. In terms of gender, since many of these castles are scenes for the incarceration and persecution of 'innocent maiden' heroines, it can be seen as a metaphor, perhaps in some cases at a less than conscious level, for the plight of women under a patriarchal regime; although at the same time it has to be said, and has been said by many critics, that despite the terrors of the castle, these heroines usually contrive to escape. This points to a huge ambiguity at the heart of the metaphor: does the castle represent a political or psychological system which is frighteningly oppressive, or does it rather represent a kind of 'test' which has to be addressed and passed on the road to maturity? And behind all this there lies the castle as a route back into a kind of late medievalism, of which Robert Browning's 'Childe Roland to the Dark Tower came' (1855) is perhaps the most notable example.

When we come across such powerful and multivalent metaphors as this, another way of referring to them is as 'symbols', but in fact the dividing line between the metaphorical and the symbolic is tentative and shifting. It could be seen as a matter of intensity or cultural spread. By dint of its frequent use in English cultural life, the lion may fairly be regarded as a symbol, but the jaguar, for example, as in Ted Hughes's poems of that name, has a less fixed set of references and is thus available for the writer to imbue with different senses and suggested meanings. This flexibility can be seen in Hughes's poem 'Second Glance at a Jaguar' (1967):

> Skinful of bowls he bowls them,
> The hip going in and out of joint, dropping the spine
> With the urgency of his hurry
> Like a cat going along under thrown stones, under cover,
> Glancing sideways, running
> Under his spine. A terrible, stump-legged waddle
> Like a thick Aztec disemboweller,
> Club-swinging, trying to grind some square
> Socket between his hind legs round,
> Carrying his head like a brazier of spilling embers,
> And the black bit of his mouth, he takes it
> Between his back teeth, he has to wear his skin out,
> He swipes a lap at a water-trough as he turns,
> Swivelling the ball of his heel on the polished spot,
> Showing his belly like a butterfly.

(Hughes 1982: 72)

Here the poem appears to be trying to depict something which is utterly non-human; the movement and the shape of the jaguar challenge all our preconceptions about mind and body. But in order to convey this image, Hughes moves among a range of metaphors. There are the 'bowls', the heavy black spheres which appear in one sense to define the jaguar's shape and movement. There is the obviously rather apposite image of the cat; in this sense the phrase 'under cover' springs out, suggesting both the jaguar's need for concealment and the idea of the jaguar as some kind of 'secret agent', as something which cannot be fully seen, or at least not until it is too late. There is the commanding metaphor of the 'Aztec disemboweller', which juxtaposes ideas of antiquity, of an apparently inhuman or inexplicable violence, and of a particular kind of art which relies on a different kind of shaping of the universe from that which is commonplace in the modern West. 'Thick', too, is perhaps a metaphorical term, conjuring not only a shape but also a certain kind of incomprehension, but we are presumably here not meant to see this as a condemnation of the jaguar's stupidity, but more as a comment on his imperviousness to the demands of human reason, his incomprehensibility to an observer who could only be there if this were a jaguar observed in a zoo, as is suggested in the mention of the 'water-trough'. It would also be possible to see 'thick' as, again, a kind of 'transferred epithet', a metaphorical device whereby characteristics are transferred from one participant in a scene to another: what if, one might ask, it is the observer who is 'thick' in the sense of being forever challenged by the impossibility of seeing the world through the jaguar's eyes?

The 'brazier of spilling embers' takes us into a different metaphorical field, whereby the jaguar becomes associated with fire and its destructive force, and this is partly continued through the association of the jaguar as something 'driven', driven as by the 'bit' in his mouth, although yet again we might have a hint of a transferred epithet here. After all, the jaguar is, above all, *not* tamed by the bit in the way in which a horse might be, so all our efforts to understand – and thereby, in a sense, to tame – the jaguar are futile. And thus we move to the final metaphor in this half of the poem, the 'belly like a butterfly', showing the inevitable vulnerability even of the jaguar, but perhaps also, through transference, of his prey.

> At every stride he has to turn a corner
> In himself and correct it. His head

Is like the worn down stump of another whole jaguar,
His body is just the engine shoving it forward,
Lifting the air up and shoving on under,
The weight of his fangs hanging the mouth open,
Bottom jaw combing the ground. A gorged look,
Gangster, club-tail lumped along behind gracelessly,
He's wearing himself to heavy ovals,
Muttering some mantrah, some drum-song of murder
To keep his rage brightening, making his skin
Intolerable, spurred by the rosettes, the Cain-brands,
Wearing the spots off from the inside,
Rounding some revenge. Going like a prayer-wheel,
The head dragging forward, the body keeping up,
The hind legs lagging. He coils, he flourishes
The blackjack tail as if looking for a target,
Hurrying through the underworld, soundless.

                                        (Hughes 1982: 72)

One of the controlling images here in this second part of the poem is that of the machine, the body like an 'engine', although the machine is a crude one, as demonstrated in the repetition of the deliberately inelegant word 'shoving'. In the attempt to make the reader understand that which is not human, some kind of translation has to happen which will enable us to achieve a parallel understanding through metaphor. The text makes another attempt at this in 'translating' the jaguar into a 'gangster', which we might see as a development from the 'Aztec disemboweller', but now perhaps brought, more frighteningly, 'closer to home'. These metaphors, then, come to seem to depend on a certain tension between the familiar and the unfamiliar, the homely and the exotic, and this exotic moment is taken further forward in the notion of the 'mantrah' and the 'drum-song', where allusions to so-called 'primitive' cultures of Asia and Africa, respectively, serve to re-conjure the jaguar's strangeness, the idea that if he speaks a language at all, it is a language incomprehensible to 'civilised' ears.

The metaphor of the 'mantrah', however, does double duty: it also reminds us of the possibility of something 'sacred' about the jaguar, something which tells us of wider and wilder stretches of creation than we might otherwise conventionally know. And this is taken forward and also returned to a more familiar Christian context in the allusion to the 'Cain-brands', the marks of killing which are here read by the poet into the markings on the jaguar's skin and fur. This, then, builds up – at the same time as returning us to the notion of the jaguar being 'under cover' – towards the final line, where the metaphor of the underworld serves at least three functions. It reminds us of the gangster, of the jaguar's hidden, 'illicit' activity, as seen through human eyes. It takes us, through Cain, into hell and thus to the hinted representation of the jaguar as an incarnation of the Devil. But, through the very hesitancy of the word 'underworld', it also reminds us of different, again more 'primitive', religions, perhaps religions based more clearly on fear of the terrors of the natural world, and of different kinds of 'underworld', of which the jaguar, at least in anthropomorphised form, may 'know' a great deal more than we do as observers.

What might also be interesting about this poem in terms of metaphor is the title, 'Second Glance at a Jaguar'. We might say literally that this is simply because Hughes had already written and published a poem called 'The Jaguar', but the word 'glance' remains arresting, signifying as it does a quick look rather than a careful inspection. The metaphor reminds us that, at least in the wild, there would be little chance of a close look at a jaguar, either because the animal would be largely invisible or because, if we were its prey, our first look might well be our last. But 'glance' also reminds us of the stock phrase, almost a cliché, a 'glancing blow', signifying a blow which does not fall directly on its target. This might refer to a jaguar's method of attack; but if so, it certainly also becomes a transferred epithet in the sense that it simulataneously refers to our attempt fully to see the jaguar, which must always fail and become only a 'sideways' attempt to apprehend something which can never be grasped in its totality. Thus, the notion of the 'glance' becomes a kind of metaphor for writing itself, which can never succeed in its self-professed task of fully incarnating its object, but must always be a mere 'glancing', momentary perception. A 'second glance', of course, could also be a way of reinspecting what has been inspected before, with a view to approaching a clearer vision of it; but this also, we suspect, is doomed to failure since, however many 'glances' at the jaguar we are afforded, they will never add up to a satisfactory picture of the whole animal, any more than a single metaphor, or even a chain of interlinked metaphors of the kind we have here, can fully grasp what is being portrayed.

I want to move to contrast the writerly assumptions behind this approach to metaphor, which in the case of Hughes is a highly self-conscious one, with a different approach to metaphor which we can find in writers in Eastern traditions. Indeed, metaphor in classical Chinese poetry can be seen to operate differently. One critic, for example, describes the role of metaphor in the poetics in ancient China thus: 'the poetics of the second century BC and its interest in metaphoricity originate in philosophising on the phenomenon of *illusion*, that is, the deceptive resemblance . . . between disparate objects, the discrepancy between appearance and actuality' (Ekstroem 2002: 1). This emphasis on illusion, while deeply rooted in Eastern philosophical and religious traditions, has something in common with the uncanny aspect of metaphor, to which I will turn in a later chapter:

> *Illusion*, thus defined, may appear as confusing or uncanny in everyday experience (the Doppelgänger, the mirage, the philanderer posing as saint, or linguistic ambiguity); yet this clash between form and content is an essential aspect of Confucian ritualism . . . observable in rules of mourning, or in the use of metaphorical poetry as ritualised discourse.
> (Ekstroem 2002: 1)

This uncanny aspect of metaphor, then, makes an early appearance in Chinese critical assumptions; what is also interesting is that the use of metaphor is here solidly grounded in a set of cultural practices, such as the 'rules of mourning' and 'ritualised discourse'. And this hints at the *constitutive* nature of metaphor in Chinese thought:

> Those who compare Western and Chinese philosophy are generally struck by the differences: formal logic never developed in China; metaphor seems to be emphasized over more rigorous argument forms in China . . . [There is an] ironical situation that Plato and Aristotle regard metaphors as second-rate tools for expressing the truth, yet they frequently invent metaphors. In contrast, Chinese thinkers express no qualms about metaphors, but often use repeatedly the same metaphors.
> (Van Norden 2004: 1–3)

This, the writer goes on to claim, is because of a fundamental distinction between Chinese and Western metaphors. In the West, metaphor has been typically used to demonstrate a correspondence between two ontologically distinct domains, but, to quote the same writer at some length, in China the situation is somewhat different:

> [The philosopher] Gaozi says that human nature is like water. Just as water will equally flow east or west depending on its environment, so will humans become good or bad depending on their environment. Mengzi [in the course of a famous debate] acknowledges that water is indifferent between east and west, but observes that it does show a preference for low over high . . . This exchange has puzzled and disappointed many interpreters, who see in the clash of metaphors empty rhetoric. However, Chinese thinkers often assume what has been called a 'correlative cosmology', according to which superficially diverse phenomena manifest the same qualitative patterns. Thus, 'the Chinese metaphor does not try to establish a parallelism between two domains, but rather wants to show that there is a *convergence* between them: the nature of water behaves in exactly the same way as the nature of man'.
>
> (Van Norden 2004: 4)

It is this concept of 'convergence' which is critical for an understanding of Chinese metaphor. Metaphor, according to this interpretation, is not a question of demonstrating human wit or ingenuity in yoking together disparate realms; rather, it is a way of revealing or explaining the convergence of things, the ways in which they tend towards a common objective, as it were, echoing each other according to a wider natural law.

To separate Eastern and Western conceptions so neatly is always to risk distortion, however. For example, it would be possible to argue that the Jesuit priest and poet Gerard Manley Hopkins's use of metaphor, devoted as it is to exposing divine intention within natural phenomena through the process Hopkins refers to as 'inscape', approximates very closely to the Chinese model:

> Glory be to God for dappled things –
>   For skies of couple-colour as a brinded cow;
>   For rose-moles all in stipple upon trout that swim;

Fresh-firecoal chestnut-falls; finches' wings;
  Landscape plotted and pieced – fold, fallow, and plough;
    And all trades, their gear and tackle and trim.

All things counter, original, spare, strange;
  Whatever is fickle, freckled (who knows how?)
    With swift, slow; sweet, sour; adazzle, dim;
He fathers-forth whose beauty is past change:
                    Praise him.
          ('Pied Beauty' in Hopkins 1990: 144)

Here, it is clearly possible to see the whole world as a vast series of metaphors for God's creation, and in this respect Hopkins is following through an aspect of biblical thinking. Everything manifests, in one form or another, some attribute of the divine; as with William Blake, the divine is at the heart of everything, and we can only grasp the 'thing-ness' of a thing by seizing upon its divine representation. Nevertheless, in Hopkins, we might say, there is a highly wrought quality to his use of metaphor; these divine attributes may be present in the phenomena of the world, perhaps God-given, according to the romantic and post-romantic tradition. But it remains the duty of the poet to find new ways to manifest in linguistic and literary form the relevance of these metaphors. We might contrast Hopkins's 'Pied Beauty' (1877) with a mid-eighth-century Chinese poem:

When a single petal falls away,
  it is spring's diminishment,
a breeze that tosses thousands of flecks
  quite makes a man dejected.

I watch them the while, till almost gone,
  blossoms passing my eyes,
weary not, though the harm be great,
  of ale that enters lips.

At river's side small manors
  Are roosts for kingfishers,
high tomb barrows by the park
  give unicorns' repose.

> Careful research on the pattern of things
>   sends men to seek delight –
> what use to let hopes of tenuous glory
>   fetter this body of mine?
>   ('Bending River' in Owen 1996: 424)

The entire metaphorical structure of this poem, written by the great Chinese poet Du Fu during the T'ang Dynasty, is devoted to establishing correspondences. At stake, at least seen from one angle, is the relation between the singular and the multiple: the 'single petal' is not merely itself; it represents, as it 'falls away', a much wider pattern, in this case the pattern of the seasons that is an enduring theme of Chinese poetry. But the question would be: what might the relationship be between these natural forces and human life? Is there some simple equation here, or is there disparity? And, perhaps more to the point, in what way do they *converge*?

There is a further metaphorical tension in the poem, between that kind of reflection that grants, or at least might grant, 'repose', and that other kind of reflection which tends rather to lean towards involvement in the world ('sends men to seek delight'). Seen from this perspective, the poem becomes a meditation upon metaphor itself, which indeed we also frequently see in the Chinese code for naming places. What, the poem seems to ask, is it to be a person? Although it should also be noted that, despite the meditative tone of the poem, this is not, as it were, an eternal question, but rather one that Du Fu is posing to himself in his specific context, as a poet recently returned to the relative safety of court in the midst of imperial battles.

The convergence, then, occurs at the point where the poet tries to assess the force and relevance of the metaphors to the particular predicament in which he finds himself, and this derives partly from the very different attitude taken by classical Chinese poets towards the question of originality. The task is not to forge new metaphors; rather, it is to reinspect the continuing relevance of old metaphors to current cultural and personal circumstances. Perhaps a clearer, although less self-reflective, example can be found in a poem written by Zhou Bang-yan to a lover in the late eleventh/early twelfth century:

> At Peach Creek I did not stay
>   enjoying myself at leisure;
> once lotus roots break in fall,
>   they never can be rejoined.
> I waited for her back then
>   on the bridge with red rails,
> and today I follow all alone
>   a path of yellowed leaves.
>
> Lines of hilltops in the mist
>   green beyond counting,
> geese turn their backs to evening sun
>   toward dusk growing redder.
> The person, like clouds coming after the wind
>   and moving onto the river;
> the passion, like floss that sticks to the ground
>   in the aftermath of rain.
>   ('Spring in the Mansion of Jade'
>   [Yu-lou chun] in Owen 1996: 577)

Here, we begin from a kind of metaphor which could be easily paralleled in Western poetry: the image of the broken root which can never be joined together again as a sign for the separation of the lovers. Whether this is a matter of mutual regret or a construction by the author, we can, as is the case with every love poem, never really know. But the overall point is that Zhou is using this repertoire of older metaphors that include most noticeably a panoply of colour coding, again based loosely on the seasons, to find some kind of convergence between the natural scene and the plight, the emotion which he is trying to develop. It needs, though, to be noted that the 'natural scene' is also anything but a natural scene, since it is deeply imbued with traditional Chinese tropes. So everything builds up, albeit extremely quietly, to the final four lines. The 'person' here, whoever or whatever it signifies, has an almost ghostly status, and thus becomes in itself a kind of metaphor for the insubstantiality of desire, which in turn is used as a metaphor for the equal insubstantiality of poetry, the impossibility of poetry, or of any other kind of writing, ever to reconstruct the object which it mourns. Yet, the poem concludes, perhaps such a reconstruction is indeed possible, but only and precisely through metaphor; perhaps the image of the 'floss that sticks to the ground/in the aftermath of rain' is an appropriate metaphor not only for the abandoned lover's plight but also for the task of poetry itself, which is to search ceaselessly for these elusive convergences between, for example, nature and artifice.

In this kind of poetry, then, there is self-conscious exercise of skill, but it is not designed to provoke awareness of strange and apparently bizarre coincidences between things, as in the manner of the metaphysical poets of the early seventeenth-century English tradition, who expressed their queries about divine rule through their ironised difficulties with scientific discoveries based on instruments which were then the new technology. It is designed rather to disclose a new and contemporary, if necessarily transient, correlation between the poet's condition and the stock of metaphors which he has inherited. Thus, we may fairly say of traditional Chinese poetry, as I have mentioned before, that it is better considered as a series of parts of a continuous process of *metaphorisation*; but the crucial point is to make this stock of metaphors *converge*, to find and reveal in them an underlying ground, so that a general term like 'passion', for example, 'takes root' in a sphere which spans natural imagery and the interior world of the poet considered as a human subject, in all the complex senses of that term.

What, though, of illusion? Perhaps at the heart of traditional Chinese metaphor there is frequently the sense that its purpose is to underline, to call attention to, the illusions by which we live. Hence the emphasis on transience, the dwelling on the past and the irrecoverable, as typically in this poem by Wang Jian, 'Passing by Lace-Crest Palace' (early ninth century):

> Its jade mansions lean at a tilt,
>   the plaster walls are bare,
> green hills in layer on layer
>   surround the palace of old.
> The Warrior Emperor went away,
>   the gossamer sleeves are gone,
> the wildflowers and butterflies
>   hold sway over winds of spring.
>   (Owen 1996: 455)

This is clearly a lament for the passing of a type of power, and of a way of life. What is perhaps more interesting, though, is the doubleness of the metaphor of 'gossamer', which simultaneously signifies a certain 'fineness' of the imperial past while reinforcing its fragility. This ambiguity, this sense of the transience of all things, even the most powerful, is carried over into the final line, where it is uncertain in quite what way the wildflowers and butterflies 'hold sway'. Is it that they are the very emanations of spring, in which case there might be within the poem a certain possibility of return, to or by the past? Or is it rather that these wildflowers and butter-flies, with their beautiful indifference to human life and power, represent a force which will forever prevent the return of that particular, other kind of spring which might mark the renewal of the pride of empire?

It is possible to argue that both meanings are present, and are held within the poem. However, the force of the metaphorical structure is not to astound the reader, but rather to provide confirmation of a sense of illusion which is already assumed to be known as common cultural ground. As one critic says, the poem conjures a 'site of absence' and thereby provides a sense that metaphor cannot, in the end, give the reader con-firmation that it has a grip on its object. What it might have instead is a grip, of some kind, on a certain mood, a certain state of emotion, akin perhaps in some ways to the Western romantic moods conjured by William Wordsworth's famous phrase 'emotion recollected in tranquillity' (Wordsworth and Coleridge 1968: 266), yet without the kind of possible redemptive status which is implicit in Wordsworth's formulation.

We have moved a long way from traditional descriptions of metaphor in terms of 'tenor' and 'vehicle' and perhaps the general point to make at this stage is that 'metaphor' itself is not a static, ahistorical term; it is not as though there is a pervasive, universal concept of metaphor which can be applied, like a template, to all ages and cultures. Rather, we need to historicise the term, to look as closely as possible at what different things might be considered to constitute metaphor under different historical, cultural and geographical circumstances. And this is before we even begin to look at the fundamental difference between different language systems which will play their parts in different definitions and usages of metaphor: the 'hieroglyphic' materiality of the Chinese language, for example, where it is still possible to see, even in its modern, stripped-down written forms, traces of the objects originally represented. In this sense, the whole operation of representation in Chinese differs from that available in alphabetical languages, and therefore the notion of metaphor and of the extent to which and the ways in which similarities among and differences between words on the printed page can relate to perceived differences and similarities among things will necessarily diverge.

3

PUBLIC METAPHOR

It is important to grasp that metaphor, however we might define it, constantly exceeds the literary even as it forms its basis; metaphor is the common substratum of the representation of institutions, corporations, public bodies. The French Marxist thinker Louis Althusser described how we are 'interpellated' through language (Althusser 1977: 162–70); that is to say, how we are constituted as subjects. We are given to believing, he said, that we are in some sense free agents, coherent subjects in our own right, when in fact we are at the mercy of an ideological flood that threatens to engulf us. Although Althusser did not say as much, we might suggest that the principal way in which we are interpellated is through metaphor, and also that we are interpellated *as* metaphor.

For example, as I open my newspaper today I see an article under the headline, 'Tobacco giants deny fraud in $280bn trial'. Now, it is obvious that tobacco companies are not actually giants, although equally it may not be easy to say what actually is a giant. What is being said here is that tobacco companies are very large, but this does not stop the flow of metaphor. For where there are giants there are giant-killers; and, as a reader of a liberal newspaper, I am being interpellated, hailed as part of a specific cultural and historical community, through this hardly remembered but still potent fairy-tale connection. I am being addressed as somebody who is on the side of the giant-killers, somebody for whom the size of the tobacco companies is itself grotesque, although this grotesquerie is in fact a compound of their size with the lethal nature of their dealings with human beings.

The 'Jack, the giant-killer' motif is actually entirely inapplicable to the story itself, which concerns a legal suit being brought against the tobacco companies not by the 'little people' implied in the metaphor but in fact by the US government. But this in no way prevents the play of metaphor: later in the story we read of a memo sent among the 'tobacco giants' saying that it was essential to provide smokers with the 'psychological crutch and some rationale to continue smoking'. The word 'crutch' in this context is obviously interesting; from being an essential device to help those with a disability, it has become here, in the communication system of the tobacco corporations, an accusation of feebleness implying contempt for their own customers. The memo was, we are told, somewhat ambiguously, 'secret'; despite this, however, one of the lawyers for the companies remains confi-dent that they will win their case because, he says, 'fraud is a very high bar'. Literally, he presumably means to imply that a successful prosecution for fraud requires a high level of proof; but the image comes from the world of sport, and implicitly by association reduces the life-or-death consequences of smoking to a game. As a final point in this single article, randomly chosen, we learn near the end that 'the courtroom battle is seen by anti-smoking advocates as the pinnacle of tobacco legislation'. All of these metaphors are commonplaces of journalism, but when added up and placed alongside a further reference to the 'pool' of smokers which is being constantly replenished to compensate for those who are 'dying off', we can perhaps begin to see what every lawyer and advertising person knows: that a 'case', whether at law or in the public mind, is as strong as the metaphors deployed to sustain it.

Metaphors, then, are integral to public life, and this is so not only at the verbal level, but also at the visual. One might consider the red rose which is the symbol of New Labour. The motivation behind the creation and adoption of this symbol, we might fairly suppose, is not merely to juxtapose but to jam together two indicators: the rose, as the symbol of Britain, or perhaps more properly of England, and the colour red signifying the, at least residual, traces of socialism in New Labour. The intention is to suggest that the natural colour of the rose is red; but this depends again on a set of metaphorical associations. Consider Blake's poem 'The Sick Rose' (1794):

Oh Rose, thou art sick!
The invisible worm
That flies in the night,
In the howling storm,

Has found out thy bed
Of crimson joy:
And his dark secret love
Does thy life destroy.
(Blake 1966: 213)

For such a short poem, this is a highly complex one. We might initially feel that the metaphorical force of the rose is traditional, signifying beauty, purity, freshness, but this is not the only interpretation possible. This rose, indeed, may well have *become* sick because of the ministrations of the lethal worm; but on the other hand, it is equally possible that the sickness of the rose is precisely its complicity with the worm. If the worm has had to 'find out' the 'bed of crimson joy', then this implies something about secretiveness, and thus that the rose may have colluded in its own corruption.

Here, at least, we are challenged to continue to accept a common belief, which is that commonplace objects have a limited range of metaphorical meanings. Even the rose, with its traditional connotations of fragrance and purity, can appear in different situations, which underlines the very important point that metaphor is primarily *contextual*. Consider, for example, an advertisement in the same issue of the newspaper which gave us 'tobacco giants'. It was for home shredding machines, under the headline 'The World's Toughest Shredders. Fight Our Fastest Growing Crime: Identity Fraud'.

There are many points one could make about this. One concerns the word 'toughest'. The metaphor by means of which the quality of these shredding machines is assured is cast, presumably not accidentally, in the context of the wider political connotations of the advertisement, in terms of the New Labour mantra 'Tough on crime; tough on the causes of crime'. By means of the metaphor, a certain level and type of modernity is proffered, and we are interpellated as citizens who wish to quell crime and who will somehow be contributing to this effort by buying a particular brand of shredder. But there is more to it than this, because current political rhetoric inexorably connects crime with asylum-seekers, those whose identity, in more than one sense, is uncertain; therefore, by joining in with this 'fight against crime', we are implicitly helping to repel an invasion, securing precisely our own identity against those who may wish or seek to encroach upon it. Thus, buying these shredders becomes, by a series of metaphorical shifts, virtually a public or patriotic duty, while at the same time it defines us as part of a community under siege. The paradox here, which is perhaps not entirely different from that in 'The Sick Rose', is that, when you think about it, the only way apparently on offer to preserve the purity of the State is through secrecy: 'The best way to protect yourself is to shred all personal information before you throw it away', the advertisement continues. Here, it is clear that shredding has itself become a metaphor; what is signified is that the State may be protective but it is also potentially intrusive, and the only way to preserve individuality is, paradoxically, to shred all evidence of it.

We might also want to consider the metaphorical structures which surround political movements. An example would be the pressure group 'Fathers4Justice', which sought to bring to people's attention the plight of fathers who were separated from the mothers of their children and regarded themselves as having inadequate access rights to those children. One of the things the name of the group might subliminally remind us of is the vast chain of toy shops formerly called 'Toys'R'Us'. By playing on this rhetoric, the group sought to establish that they are nice, friendly people, who fully understand children's needs and wish to play their part in infant upbringing. This is supported by the symbol '4', which matches with the symbol 'R', but also calls to mind a realm of text messaging which again reassures the recipient of the message that this is a phenomenon which is thoroughly in tune with the young. But one of the principal methods the group used to bring themselves and their complaint to public attention was by dressing up as superheroes, a metaphor which works in several ways. In the first place, it underlines the notion that fathers are fully in touch with the world of their children. But because one of the facts about superheroes is that they are, at least in part, out of date, this is also designed to show that fathers retain their own memories of childhood, a detail designed to make the recipient of the metaphor feel closer to them and to incite sympathy. Then again, the notion of the superhero works in quite different way, to remind us of the 'heroism' of the male; this is designed less to incite sympathy than to command respect. And finally, although there are certainly further connotations, the notion of the super-hero returns full circle, because by dressing up and performing such stunts as climbing tall buildings, a certain irony comes into the equation: fathers, we are being implicitly told, are not merely serious persons deserving of respect; they are simultaneously able to laugh at themselves and at their own pretensions. They are serious yet playful.

Another contemporary example would be the Countryside Alliance. The word 'countryside' carries its own ideological weight: it conjures up a slightly old-fashioned view of rural life, which implicitly bolsters the Alliance's claim to represent a traditional way of life which is under threat from the forces of modernisation. 'Alliance', similarly, carries ideological baggage. An 'alliance', according to one of its dictionary definitions, is 'people united by kinship or friendship'; thus, the Countryside Alliance hopes to mark itself off from the common run of political parties or movements and to establish itself in the public mind as a loose group of like-minded people who, in the context of this looseness and friendliness of affiliation, represent in themselves the way of life in the countryside and thus become precisely an emblem for the communal habits and charac-teristics they claim to seek to preserve.

All public life sustains itself through metaphors. The recently redevel-oped centre of the city of Bristol, for example, is marked by two enormous sculptures, known as 'the Sails', which, through particular arrangements of metal and fabric, resemble the sails of a ship and thus serve to act as a metaphor for Bristol's maritime past. Such a public metaphor seeks to control and restrict a chain of associations: it does not seek to remind us of the less currently acceptable aspects of this past – the slave trade, for example, or the trade in tobacco – but rather to play upon folk memories of sailing ships, of early explorers, of the danger, risk, thrill and adventure of life at sea in a rather less than specific period of history. The French thinker and critic Roland Barthes, in his famous essay 'Myth Today' (1957), referred to the whole collection of Western representations of China as 'sinity' (Barthes 1973: 121); following this thread, we might refer to this chain of associations in Bristol under the heading 'maritimity'. The most prestigious and influential commercial society in Bristol lays further claim to this set of historical associations by continuing to call itself the 'Merchant Venturers', and we can see a related rhetoric on a national scale with the advent of companies of risk funders referring to themselves under the heading 'Venture Capital'. Here again, there are demarcations around the word 'venture', which has a curious range of apparent meanings, from the timidity underlined in the phrase 'I venture to suggest that . . .' to the boldness implicit in the idea of 'venturing' onto the open seas, or into a theatre of danger.

What does this reveal about the general position of metaphor? It shows that metaphor is never static, and rarely innocent. A particularly interesting example in current speech, although a complex one to discuss, is the presence of the word 'like' in contemporary youth jargon. An example would be, 'I was, like, what is going on here?', a kind of speech which is brilliantly parodied in the television series *Little Britain*. What is happening here is, in one sense, a kind of act of impersonation. Rather than simply reporting on the past, the word 'like' introduces what appears to be an actual recounting of how the person felt, what he or she was thinking, at the time. The complexity derives from the fact that the word 'like' is traditionally supposed to introduce precisely, as we have seen, a type of metaphor, a simile, but the use here has been subtly changed and one could argue that this also touches on the eruption of notions of virtual reality into everyday life. We might paraphrase the structure as implying, 'I did not actually think that; but it was "as though" I had thought that'. In a metaphorical usage like this, while in one sense past habits of speech may appear to grow closer and more vivid, they also become curiously intangible, reflecting wider cultural and social difficulties with public and private memory in an age when access to information through the worldwide web is virtually instantaneous and there is consequently little need to rely on the vagaries of personal remembrance. It could also be that there is a reference to a certain fragmentation of the self, to which I shall return in a moment.

In this sense metaphor is a crucial aspect of power; the control of public metaphor is a way of gaining and securing power. One may reasonably think of the still frequent use of the term 'the Crown' to signify the control of British society by royalty. And perhaps the most revealing metaphor in British cultural life shows up under this heading, namely the apparent fact that in the United Kingdom, as opposed to, say, in the United States or France, we are all conventionally referred to as 'subjects' of the monarch. It is perhaps critical to pause on this for a moment. I have referred to the term 'subject' several times now, and for many years it has been a crucial term in theoretical discourse, as I have hinted in my remarks on Althusser above. One of the results of this theoretical attention has been to criticise, even deconstruct or dismember, the term and thereby to expose its inner contradictions.

Put very briefly, the notion of the subject appears at first glance to presuppose something unified, whether this be in terms of the 'subject of an utterance', which means the person doing the uttering, or the subject of, for example, a conversation, in which case it refers to the apparent topic of such a conversation. But when one looks more closely at the word, especially in the political context, one is also referred back to its Latin root, as something or someone which is 'thrown under', as in the modern usage of 'subjected to'. The word 'subject' therefore alludes at the same time to a kind of unificatory power *and* to powerlessness, subservience. A poem by Dannie Abse, 'A Suburban Episode' (1968), begins with the following two stanzas:

> Since you telephoned to say – in a tiny voice –
> (how servile you are) intruders intruders walk
> in pairs across the back lawn (I'm sorry, you say)
> I say heartily, too heartily perhaps,
> do not lock yourself in oh dear no,
> go out, shout, challenge them, ask them why.
>
> Since you say that some – the most impertinent –
> and therefore you think (wrongly) the most important,
> for instance, those in plum-coloured blazers,
> are cutting down your tulips, snip snip snip,
> one by one with small scissors, small nail-scissors,
> I say with formidable aggression
> stride out, ask them for credentials, stop them;
> but remember walk with very long steps.
>
> (Abse 1977: 104)

It would be fair to say that what we have here is a sustained series of metaphors of public power and the powerlessness of the subject, but most of the metaphors contain or enact a certain ambiguity. To take just one example: the phrase 'tiny voice' in the first line has multiple referents. It could be that the voice is fairly literally 'tiny' in the sense of being very quiet or soft, although even here there is a metaphor at work, since the most obviously literal referent of 'tiny' is to physical size, and that is not a property which a voice can have. It could also, however, be that the narrator of the poem, whom we assume to be a man, regards the voice as 'tiny' because it seems to him comparatively insignificant, compared, for example, with the exaggerated 'heartiness' of his own response. It could also simply be 'tiny' because it is coming through a telephone, which might be seen as reducing volume, although here the question of how small a voice one might hear on a telephone is again a matter of power, since it is within the power of the hearer to adjust the distance between telephone and ear. But when we consider metaphor, we have also to consider not only the word itself, but also the adjacent possibilities of the word: so that 'tiny' might quite easily become 'tinny', which again could be seen either as a telephonic effect or as an implicit criticism by the narrator of the caller's voice, and hence of her – if we assume it to be a woman – complaint. If her complaint is 'tinny', then by a metaphorical extension we may consider it to be without foundation, without substance, hollow and rattling; but as we consider this, whether consciously or unconsciously, we are also therefore forming a judgement of how the narrator is receiving this call and what judgements he himself is bringing to bear on the caller.

Thus, an entire satire on the way bureaucracy deals with complaints or, indeed, desperate appeals, is already being formed in this first crucial metaphor. In the second stanza we might similarly think about the 'plum-coloured blazers'. The blazers themselves might well be a metaphor for a certain type of old-fashioned power or authority, and here again we may wish to pause for a moment and consider whether dress, fashion, the way of bedecking the human body is itself a type of metaphor. It is noticeable, for example, in television news broadcasts that Western male politicians and diplomats dress very differently from their counterparts from different cultures. The typical Western male dress, including suit, tie and belt, serves metaphorically to create a sense of completeness and power; jackets are cut to fit an exaggerated version of the male physique (and the notion of 'power-dressing' for women, which usually involves padded shoulders and nipped-in waists, enacts the same scenario). Within this regime, power surges upwards to create a looming body which asserts its power through the strength of its shoulders and marks its boundaries carefully with sharp and clearly defined shapes and edges. There are many other forms of dress with which one could contrast this. To take one example, the Arabic djellaba provides no interior padding or shaping of any kind; it simply falls from the shoulders to cover the entire body without emphasising any particular feature of it. One could take this further by looking at the content of fashion sales catalogues: whereas in the West the emphasis is on clarity of line and, quite often and especially for women, exposure or accentuation of key bodily features, in catalogues for Arabic wear the emphasis is on covering, on removing the shape of the body from the gaze. In fact, this goes one step further, because in orthodox Islamic clothing catalogues, because of the taboo on the portrayal of the human form or face, the models have no heads. This, then, is also a version of public metaphor, a way in which an apparently minor cultural code carries a weightier signification.

To return to Dannie Abse and the 'plum-coloured blazers': the blazers themselves metaphorically signify membership of a club, class or caste. It is obviously one from which the caller considers herself to be excluded, whether by reason of gender or otherwise. However, the plum colouring reminds us of other things again, such as the metaphor of a 'plummy' accent, which was probably originally derived from the sense of the speaker having a 'plum in his mouth' but is now more broadly applied in class contexts. It may or may not be relevant to this specific context, but it is worth remembering that P.G. Wodehouse, the arch-chronicler of the early twentieth-century upper classes, was known as 'Plum'; ostensibly because as a small child this was the closest he got to pronouncing his own first name, Pelham, but we may suspect that the ongoing metaphor runs deeper than that.

The final stanza of the poem extends the series of metaphors and disturbs them, as the narrator makes us aware of the menace even he feels at least partly as a result of his caller's experience:

Do not apologise. For believe me
I believe you. I know your nation (I mean your nature)
and how cunning things can be, damnably cunning.
Why, have I not heard, even I, first cousin
of the mayor, heard in the night a stone falling?
No ordinary stone either, scraping the sheer ledges,

and later many stones, boulders even, leaping down
out of earshot, down the sides of hell.

(Abse 1977: 105)

The pun on 'nation' and 'nature' reveals to the reader, at the very least, an implicit racism in the narrator. More importantly, though, what the stanza shows is a version of the disintegration of the subject; we come to feel ourselves to be in the presence of a character who is not, as he has claimed, immune to fear, but rather concerned with covering up and dismissing his fears. Hell here clearly serves a metaphorical purpose, of revealing to us the notion of a feared void within the narrator, a point at which all his apparent bureaucratic and official certainties no longer convince.

Thus, we have a set of metaphors on the terrain of power and powerlessness and of the ability of the subject to remain, or ever to be, in control of his or her own life, and we may speculate that this too is of the very essence of metaphor. Metaphor, of course, consists of comparison, but perhaps these comparisons can never be quite equal; perhaps they always also serve some purpose of aggrandisement or belittlement. And the notion of 'belittlement' can take us further into the relationship between public metaphor, power and childhood. We might pursue the theme of the telephone as metaphor, for distance, for incomprehension, for a type of communication which is, in a crucial way, unnatural. Sylvia Plath's well-known poem 'Daddy' (1962) contains the lines:

So daddy, I'm finally through.
The black telephone's off at the root,
The voices just can't worm through.

(Plath 1981: 224)

Here, the metaphorical structure involves an implicit comparison between the telephone and the voice, or voices, of the dead. The narrator of 'Daddy' is haunted by her father in a way which, we might suggest, is perennially applicable if we accept that the 'voices' we hear in our childhood, the voices of authority and power, never leave us but continue to inform our day-to-day actions and decisions. The fact of the narrator's father's death in no way affects this power over the subject; at least, that is what we might think while reading the poem up to this moment, when the assertion is made that the narrator has actually succeeded in 'killing the dead'. When she says, 'I'm finally through', it would seem that the force of the metaphor is double, and indeed more than double, it is virtually paradoxical: on the one hand, it implies that communication has been established, in the sense of having been 'put through' by the telephone exchange to the potential hearer; but, on the other hand, it implies that she is 'finished' with her father. This is confirmed in the final stanza, which also picks up on much further metaphor in the poem about Nazis, vampires and other creatures of evil and the night:

> There's a stake in your fat black heart
> And the villagers never liked you.
> They are dancing and stamping on you.
> They always *knew* it was you.
> Daddy, daddy, you bastard, I'm through.
>
> (Plath 1981: 224)

From one point of view, one could say that the accumulation of metaphors here and throughout the poem is designed to permit the formation of a whole subject. The father is presented as what we might call constant interference on the line, as a voice, whether imagined or remembered, which is constantly preventing the subject from reaching a condition of entirety. Thus, by associating the father metaphorically with Nazism and vampirism, the self of the poem, which is presented as a kind of child-self, is seeking to use metaphor as a mode of explanation and also as a way of developing from a subjected position. To be 'through' is not only to be connected; it is also, in a quite different way, to have survived that condition. Furthermore, it is to be on the point of death, and so we may suspect that the metaphors run two ways: towards the evolution of a real power in the subject, but simultaneously towards an acknowledgement that such power will be deathly because it is only by accepting or otherwise dealing with the notion that the self, the subject, has been formed by others that one can come to an understanding of the individual's inescapable dependency on his or her own past.

It would now be possible, following one line of thought, to begin to see metaphor as that which 'stands in' for the human absence which marks and defines the subject of capitalist world-formation. The notion of resistance through remetaphorisation, through what the French thinkers Gilles Deleuze and Félix Guattari called a 'reterritorialisation' of conquered realms (Deleuze and Guattari 1988: 111–48), becomes a substrate of literary resistance itself. We might see it, for example, in the major literary theorist Maurice Blanchot's insistence on the inextricability of literature and death, in Samuel Beckett's refusal of elaborated discourse, or in Salman Rushdie's insistence on excess of speech as recompense for the refusal of the 'native' language. Perhaps the case of Beckett is particularly worth mentioning, as an example of a writer who, in one sense, resists the elaborations of metaphor, at least in part because of their contamination by public discourse. We might hypothesise that this is precisely why many of his characters experience difficulties with reality as it is usually presented to them. For example, in the 'Magdalen Mental Mercyseat' chapter in the novel *Murphy* (1938), reality is an altogether difficult matter, not to be apprehended by the normal means of comparison and translation but far more elusive:

> The nature of outer reality remained obscure. The men, women and children of science would seem to have as many ways of kneeling to their facts as any other body of illuminati. The definition of outer reality, or of reality short and simple, varied according to the sensibility of the definer. But all seemed agreed that contact with it, even the layman's muzzy contact, was a rare privilege.
>
> (Beckett 1973: 101)

We are a long way here from that condition of metaphor in which the poet, the writer or the advertiser can point to two phenomena and advise us that they have similarities. We are instead in a world where the common ground of such comparisons, the conviction that all of us, or at least all of us in some specific 'interpretive community', to quote the literary theorist Stanley Fish's phrase (Fish 1980), share common assumptions is no longer obvious, if it ever has been. The 'Magdalen Mental Mercyseat' is itself a marvellously satirical composite of metaphors. 'Magdalen' comes from a whole Christian and, in the Irish context of Beckett and *Murphy*, Catholic tradition. The word 'Mental', in this context, signifies the power of a 'scientific' establishment to classify people as 'mentally ill', as 'patients'.

'Mercyseat' takes us back in a sense to the religious register of metaphor, but in another way reminds us of the function of metaphor as euphemism, with something in it about the evasion of the dreadful facts of mental ill-health, incarceration and, eventually, death.

The passage itself continues this violent mixture of metaphors. There are the scientists; there are the 'illuminati', the mention of whom suggests to us that perhaps so-called scientific rigour is not quite what it seems; and there is the kneeling, which again takes us back to church. Beckett's purpose in using these metaphors is, to employ a term which was often utilised when describing his drama, 'absurd': it is not that he wants his reader to gain new direct knowledge through these experiences and comparisons; it is rather that he wants to emphasise the vast variety of holds on reality according to which people live their lives, the disparity between the public formations and metaphors of institutions such as the Church and the mental health profession, and the struggle of the individual as he or she strives to find metaphors which actually work as they try to grasp the world around them.

This might lead us to think about Beckett's famous play *Waiting for Godot* (1955), and especially because here is a play which 'plays' to the utmost on a resistance to metaphorisation. The characters Vladimir and Estragon are, at least patchily, engaged in a struggle to discover meaning in the situation in which they find themselves and in the events which occasionally befall them, as well as in their hazy recollections of the past; but this never proves possible. And neither does it prove any more possible for readers and critics than it does for the characters themselves. The stage set for *Waiting for Godot* contains a single central object, a withered tree. It would seem obvious that, given its extraordinary prominence, it serves some kind of metaphorical function; but what kind? Does it represent a certain kind of barrenness, the hopelessness about change which is the lot of the two characters? Does it represent, on the contrary, the hope, however vestigial, of new life? Does it represent the already metaphorised 'tree' which is a synonym for the cross of Jesus Christ's crucifixion? Does it, in some sense, represent for Vladimir and Estragon the entire world, since there are no other objects or directions from which they can get their bearings?

All of these things are possible; but the point should probably be that the tree, in its barrenness, its reluctance to yield any kind of secret meaning, instead represents the *exhaustion* of metaphor. We shall come on to psychological and psychoanalytic readings of metaphor later; but we might say that one thing *Waiting for Godot* suggests is that the very process of constructing and understanding metaphor requires a certain energy in the life around us, which is the deeper ground behind the complexities of perception and reflection. For Vladimir and Estragon this energy is only sporadically available, and our fear at the end of the play is that this is unlikely to change. There is a name for the condition where the whole world seems as bleak as a withered tree and where there seems no possibility of escape from the unending and repetitive present. In fact, there are several names for it. Coleridge knew it, emblematically, in 'Dejection: An Ode' (1802) as dejection,

> A grief without a pang, void, dark, and drear,
>   A stifled, drowsy, unimpassioned grief,
>   Which finds no natural outlet, no relief,
>   In word, or sigh, or tear –
>   (Coleridge 1967: 364)

And what he finds is that this mood, or condition, stifles his ability to 'metaphorise' the world:

> All this long eve, so balmy and serene,
> Have I been gazing on the western sky,
>   And its peculiar tint of yellow green:
> And still I gaze – but with how blank an eye!
>   (Coleridge 1967: 364)

Coleridge's dejection is manifested to him as an inability to make connections, to see more deeply into the heart of difference and similarity. We might reasonably say that there is a paradox in the poem since, while he is bemoaning his lack of imagination, he is nevertheless writing a brilliantly metaphorical poem. Another variant of the state would be 'melancholy'. But, to take this back to *Waiting for Godot*, the word we now more often use for this mood is 'depression': a sense of being stuck, of being unable to move outside ourselves in order to participate in the outer world, or even to manipulate it to our view. The poet Les Murray, among others including Winston Churchill, refers to it as 'the black dog' (Murray 1997).

Depression perhaps gives us a window through which to look at what it might be like to live in a non-metaphorical world. There are indeed people who live in such a world all the time, people whose mental illness consigns them to chronically 'concrete thought', which I shall consider in more detail in a later chapter; but if we consider depression to be a kind of 'retreat', or defile, in the continuous activity of metaphorising that makes us human, then this will open up the notion of metaphor as an essential ground of human activity.

However, to come back to 'public metaphor', there is clearly a two-edged sword at play here. On the one hand, our freedom to metaphorise is an essential aspect of our more general human freedom. If we think, to paraphrase Hamlet for rather different purposes, that a cloud looks very like a camel, we are free in a democratic society to say so, and at least to offer this perception to others, even if they disagree. But if, on the other hand, we see a picture of a camel on a pack of cigarettes called, unsurprisingly, 'Camel', then we are not free: we are constrained in our perception. We may choose to accept the implicit metaphor being offered, even if it might be very difficult to see quite what it is, other than the notion of a cigarette being an 'oasis-like' form of relief, or of a cigarette somehow reminding us of exotic Eastern mysteries, or of a cigarette being somehow a way of getting us, like a 'ship of the desert', through difficult times. Or we may choose to ignore it. Whichever we do, it is not going to go away; it is part of the huge system of 'embedded metaphor' which surrounds us at every point of our social lives, and with which we are dealing in one way or another at every moment.

4

METAPHOR AND THE 'TEXT INSTEAD'

It might now be possible, in the light of what I have already said, to move to consider the whole of the literary text under the heading of 'metaphor', in the specific sense of a question: of asking whether the text is always in some rather peculiar – or uncanny – sense other than itself, whether it stands in not only for an absent referent but also for the body of textuality which it is not. What we need to consider is whether the text would thus be the metaphorical condensation of a host of failed or obscured alternatives; it would stand at a crossroads of identifications, as the obfuscation of a broader and less definite metaphorical field which is held down, staked out on the model of what might be considered an 'imperial' reterritorialisation of textual lands wrongly perceived as previously unpeopled. This might appear abstruse, but consider what happens when we describe a scene or tell an anecdote to others; often we might prearrange what we are about to tell, or how we are about to tell it. There would have been dozens of other ways in which we might choose to recount the incident; the one we choose is designed to maximise the force of what has impressed us. Just so – yet, obviously, even more so – with the written text. Seen in this light, we might thus say that metaphor in the Western sense becomes itself a metaphor *of* 'Western sense', inextricably involved with linguistic and cultural choices, hierarchies (which might themselves be seen as colonialisms, in the sense that the implications of hierarchy are always to do with establishing what is taken to be at the centre and what is at the margin). In pursuing this idea, the thinking behind this chapter will be to do with deconstruction, and I will introduce briefly one or two of the things Jacques Derrida has to say about metaphor, giving examples of what a deconstructive approach to specific metaphorical examples would look like.

We can begin by looking at a remarkable book, *Life of Pi* by Yann Martell, which was published in Britain in 2002 and won the Man Booker Prize in that year. *Life of Pi* tells the story of a young Indian who is the son of a zookeeper. With his parents and a collection of the zoo's animals, he embarks on a Japanese-registered ship bound for the United States, where the zoo is to be reopened. In the middle of the trip the ship unexpectedly, inexplicably and very swiftly sinks. Pi ends up on a lifeboat; no other human beings survive, as far as he knows, but on the boat are a hyena and a wounded zebra. The hyena eats the zebra, and subsequently also kills and eats an orang-utan which arrives on the boat. Meanwhile, however, the boy becomes aware that, beneath the boat's awning, there is another creature on board, a tiger. The bulk of the book consists of descriptions of ways in which Pi manages to avoid being killed by the tiger, principally by building a rather shaky raft which he attaches to the boat, and on which he can live while the tiger has free rein on the boat itself.

Eventually, the boat and the raft arrive on the coast of Mexico, where the tiger escapes and Pi is found and taken to Canada, where, as he says, 'my story ends' (Martell 2002: 286). But the most interesting part of the book is that his story does not end there. There is a further part, set in the Mexican infirmary where he is initially taken, in which he is interrogated by two men working on behalf of the Japanese ship's owners, who are trying to discover why the ship sank in the first place. In Chapter 96 Pi is asked to tell his story. Chapter 97 consists of two words, 'The story' (Martell 2002: 291), which refers, one must suppose, to the preceding ninety-six chapters.

However, the Japanese questioners do not believe his story; they claim that it is impossible and that, in effect, they want a different story. They say they want one 'without animals' (Martell 2002: 303), so Pi tells them one. In many ways it replicates the narrative of the original story, but now the zebra has become an injured sailor, the hyena has become a brutal ship's cook, and the orang-utan has become Pi's mother. The major problem which this new story causes the investigators is that if this analysis is correct, then what it also implies, from his own account, is that Pi must himself fit into the only remaining narrative slot, namely that of the tiger.

The relevance of this to metaphor perhaps needs some clarification. The question is: is Pi's original account of events, which occupies the bulk of the book and which is theoretically replicated in Chapter 97, a metaphor, or a set of metaphors? It would obviously be easy to explain it in this way. We might say, for example, that Pi has indeed survived a ghastly journey, with the other survivors murderously attacking each other because of hunger and despair, and during the course of which he himself has eventually turned murderer and killed the bloodthirsty cook. Traumatised by these events, he has concocted a metaphorised account of them to protect himself from both his new insights into man's inhumanity to man and also his own sense of guilt and terror at what he has done. Thus, the story, like many other stories of survival, should not be taken literally but rather read as an allegory, which is one form, as we have seen, of extended metaphor: an allegory of a quite different set of events.

Alternatively, we might say that Pi offers his second version of the story only because he is sadly aware that his original account is not being believed, and is not likely to be believed. If this were the case, then the process of metaphorisation would work the other way round: the second story would be an attempt to produce within the first narrative the kind of meaning which others can understand; it would be an attempt to 'naturalise' a series of events which would otherwise remain inexplicable.

The book does end with a kind of resolution, in the form of the final paragraph of the otherwise inconclusive report which the Japanese write as a result of their encounter with Pi:

> As an aside, story of sole survivor, Mr Piscine Molitor Patel, Indian citizen, is an astounding story of courage and endurance in the face of extraordinarily difficult and tragic circumstances. In the experience of this investigator, his story is unparalleled in the history of shipwrecks. Very few castaways can claim to have survived so long at sea as Mr Patel, and none in the company of an adult Bengal tiger.
>
> (Martell 2002: 319)

This would seem to imply a residual belief in Pi's original story, and one which, after all, the reader has little choice but to share since it is precisely that story which has been told throughout the book, that story whose twists and desperations we have been involved in following. We may have been on the lookout for metaphor but we have nevertheless been most deeply involved with a story in which a tiger is, actually, a tiger. As a further aside, it is worth mentioning that the tiger is called 'Richard Parker'; the reason for this is that there was a confusion when he was found as a cub along with his dead mother, and various forms were filled in wrongly, resulting in him acquiring the name of the white hunter who found him. Thus, throughout the book there is a continuing trace of further metaphorisation: are we in fact looking at a postcolonial text in which the most violent of the predators actually represents white colonialism? But if we are, what are we to make of the second story, in which, apparently, Pi himself is revealed as the tiger of his imagination?

What, at all events, we can say here is that we are confronted with a remarkable metaphorical phenomenon which I would like to refer to under the heading 'the text instead'. This phenomenon tends to make the reader wonder, first, whether what is being read is metaphorical at all; and, second, whether in some sense the entire text is a metaphor for something else, something 'unwritten' but perpetually haunting the words on the page. This would appear to be a specific effect of postmodernism, by which I mean to refer to a type of writing which is continually more or less explicitly engaged with the conditions of its own textuality. For the postmodern text, nothing is taken for granted; at its most extreme, there is no extra-textual 'real' to which the text might refer, and this 'absence of validation' itself becomes the very substance or ground of writing.

A further, and rather different, example would be a novel by the cyber-fiction writer William Gibson, *Pattern Recognition* (2003). This is a book with an enormous complexity of plot. I will begin by singling out one strand. This concerns a set of puzzling images which show up on computer screens across the world. Grainy, disconnected, black-and-white, of dubious meaning and of no known origin or provenance, they nevertheless exert an almost hypnotic power. People begin devoting large parts of their lives to developing and entertaining hypotheses about the 'footage', as these images become known. Some believe them to be slowly released excerpts from a lost or forgotten master-work of film; some believe them to be a new, or perhaps newly discovered, work by a master *auteur*; others believe them to be a work in progress which is being released at the same time as it is progressively being made.

Here, obviously, there is a key metaphor for the creative process, especially in the specific technological context of the twenty-first century. Perhaps even more there is a metaphor for the notion of criticism itself, with echoes of Barthes's theory of the 'death of the author' (Barthes 1977: 142–8) underpinning a set of reflections on how impossible it is to assign any meaningful 'authorship' to the footage. If the footage is in some sense metaphorical itself, then it is only so through the interpretive efforts of the reader; and the reader can never come upon an originary or conclusive 'meaning' for this slowly unfolding and, for all anyone knows, eternal text.

As the search goes on, a kind of 'techno-watermark' is discovered on the various pieces of the footage; it is in the form of what looks like a map, with a strange, asymmetrical mark down the centre, but efforts to discover whether it is the map of an existing city come to no avail. Eventually, by a process of discovery too complex to recount here, the footage is traced to two Russian sisters. One, Stella, has been putting the footage on the internet in order to publicise the work of the other, Nora. It transpires that Nora was long ago injured in a terrorist attack and has lost all her faculties and desires, except for the ability to work in video. This she does, very slowly producing the footage, which turns out to have to do with the event which maimed her; more intriguing, and more important, is the origin of the 'watermark', which is a precise image of the fragment of shrapnel which is still lodged in the centre of Nora's brain, and has proved impossible to remove. The whole effort of the footage has, in a sense, been predicated on the appalling asymmetry of brain – and mind – from which Nora now suffers; it is a kind of extroversion of her own wound, her own pain and suffering. The sense of freedom and joy which followers of the footage experience is evidently related, but in some inexpressible way, to the way in which this reverberates with the conditions of their own lives.

What has this to do with metaphor? It is an example, I suggest, of the specific twist which the extended metaphor takes under postmodern conditions. Where the classical metaphor posits the possibility of furthering the search for meaning through aligning one object, word or phenomenon with another, this variant on the postmodern metaphor takes as its ground the impossibility of assigning meaning. The shape of the piece of shrapnel, the shape of Nora's wound, the shape of the 'watermark', all of these are clearly related; but they do not serve to enliven or elucidate some meaningful correlation; rather, they seek to underline the controlling nature of the arbitrary.

It is perhaps worth adding that this phenomenon of the arbitrary nature of the metaphor, which follows naturally from poststructuralist thinking about the general arbitrariness of language and the sign, is also addressed in a second way in *Pattern Recognition*. The heroine, Cayce, makes her living from a peculiar talent she has – being able to spot what fashion brands are likely to be successful in the world market place. For this, naturally, she is very highly paid; but the text asserts that this is not so much a skill as the outcome of a pathological condition, which causes her physical nausea and worse in the presence of brands which are not 'of the moment'. Her very character, therefore, is built upon the evanescent, if such a thing can be. Cayce is not the first of Gibson's protagonists to be similarly named: a man named Case was the hero of the most well known of his novels, *Neuromancer* (1984), which prompts the question, 'Case of what?' What might these characters be cases of? Are they, for instance, examples of something broader, or is it the *case* that to try to assign metaphorical meaning of this kind is doomed?

In using the term 'the text instead' about this novel, what we might have in mind is the way in which 'pattern recognition' becomes a substitute or replacement for classical theories of metaphor. Instead of saying, 'This thing is like this, isn't it?', which is the assumed rhetorical move of metaphor, and is designed to change and increase our perception of the world, what is being said here is that there are arbitrary, random patterns which run through things. This, perhaps, is the polar opposite of Hopkins's view. However, having said that, it is also interesting that *Pattern Recognition* is, in the end, a recuperative text. Although not directly as a result of her recognition of the pattern, Cayce is still healed of her pathology in the end, allowed to recommence a more 'normal' life freed from the neurasthenia which has been her problem but also the source of her originality.

But there are other versions of 'the text instead', other attempts to think and write through what we might deem a conventional account and to offer another, different account which throws up new metaphors for the human condition for our inspection. Some of these attempts might be considered to fall within what was, for a little while, called the 'Martian' school of poetry, because it involved adopting a self-consciously distanced attitude towards human affairs. But far better than anything produced by the 'Martians' is a poem by the Scottish writer Edwin Morgan, 'From the Domain of Arnheim' (1968), parts of which read as follows:

And so that all these ages, these years
we cast behind us, like the smoke-clouds
dragged back into vacancy when the rocket springs –

The domain of Arnheim was all snow, but we were there.
We saw a yellow light thrown on the icefield
from the huts by the pines, and laughter came up
floating from a white corrie
miles away, clearly.
We moved on down, arm in arm.
I know you would have thought it was a dream
but we were there. And those were trumpets –
tremendous round the rocks –
while they were burning fires of trash and mammoths' bones.
They sang naked, and kissed in the smoke.
A child, or one of their animals, was crying.
Young men blew the ice crystals off their drums.
We came down among them, but of course
they could see nothing, on their time-scale.
Yet they sensed us, stopped, looked up – even into our eyes.
To them we were a displacement of the air,
a sudden chill, yet we had no power
over their fear. If one of them had been dying
he would have died. The crying
came from one just born: that was the cause
of the song. We saw it now. What had we stopped
but joy?
I know you felt
the same dismay, you gripped my arm, they were waiting
for what they knew of us to pass.
A sweating trumpeter took

a brand from the fire with a shout and threw it
where our bodies would have been –
we felt nothing but his courage.
And so they would deal with every imagined power
seen or unseen.
There are no gods in the domain of Arnheim.

We signalled to the ship; got back;
our lives and days returned to us, but
haunted by deeper souvenirs than any rocks or seeds.
From time the souvenirs are deeds.

(Morgan 1985: 42–4)

This poem is about a strange moment of engagement between humanity and a different species, coming in on a ship from space. The differences are well marked: members of the other species do not have bodies, or at least if they do, then they are not being inhabited on this occasion. Similarly, the timescale of these alien beings is different from the conventional human timescale. As a metaphorical structure, this poem offers a set of comments on the human condition; and in one sense it could be said that these metaphors are purely romantic: the 'courage', for example, of the trumpeter pointlessly throwing a brand at an intruder, or as he might see it at an enemy who cannot even be seen, let alone scared or ignited.

But there are also other levels. For example, the occasion of this visitation is of a human birth, and so it would be difficult not to interpret the poem as a 'different' account, as a 'text instead', about the birth of Jesus, and about the signs and portents which were supposed to have accompanied this birth, as they have been said to have done in the case of many figures in other religious traditions. Alternatively, we might say that the poem is a kind of metaphor for divisions within the human psyche itself: as there are the cold but courageous bodies trying to survive amid the 'icefields', at the mercy of signs which they cannot begin to understand, there are also souls, or something akin to souls, which, although they are in one sense part of those bodies, are also observing them from some kind of distance, are not totally implicated in the bodies' actions.

The consideration of Morgan's poem would be greatly deepened if we were to reflect on the fact that the title and indeed the scenario of the poem emerge from a short story by Edgar Allan Poe, 'The Domain of Arnheim' (1850), which, to put it extremely simply, is a metaphor for escape from the contingencies and trammels of the physical human realm into a constructed spiritual landscape. This is here transmuted into the landscape from which the character or characters in Morgan's poem are observing the Earth. However, the point here is more about the power of metaphor to 'reverse the terms of the equation'; thus, the reader is placed, if only transitorily, on the side of these superhuman beings, as an observer of a type of conventional life perceived as prehistoric, as in the 'mammoths' bones', although the further reference to 'Arnhem', as the site of a massive Second World War parachute drop, is also clearly relevant.

This use of metaphor, then, is one which challenges (although it can never truly transgress) the limits of what it means to be a human reader. What would it be like, Morgan implicitly asks, to see through the eyes of the 'truly other', how much sense, or what kind of sense, would human life have if it were seen according to a different scheme, or indeed bereft of the metaphors by which it is usually lived? We might notice that Morgan does not go too far here. For example, the narrator of the poem, although he might not seem initially sure that the scene he is observing is one of rejoicing, certainly does seem fully conscious of what a trumpeter is. This could mean at least two things: either that trumpeters are common, or at least known, in his own race or species, which might seem highly improbable; or that some prior observation of Earth has told him at least something of what the presence of a trumpeter might portend. Either way, the important thing narratologically is that such difficulties can only be negotiated within reasonable limits: to go too far along the metaphorical chain, to suggest the truly outlandish, in every sense of that term, would be to move too far from linguistic norms, would be to sacrifice the difficult terrain of translatability and place the reader in an impossibly convoluted position.

A final point on this poem would be to suggest that it is a sustained metaphor about power and powerlessness. The 'different' race is clearly superior to our own in terms of technology, and possibly also of observational power; but because of their lack of bodies, perhaps their purely intellectual interest, they are also inferior in power: they cannot intervene in human affairs.

A similar metaphor can be found running through, for example, many of Doris Lessing's science-fiction novels, including the *Canopus in Argos* series (1979–83); but in a sense it also runs through the whole mainstream of science fiction, so that the condition of being human is regarded as being both privileged by and at the mercy of an emotional field which is denied to the 'other', whether that other be alien, robot or a vastly superior species. The general effect of this privileged cultural metaphor, which also has its own political ramifications, is to produce a post-romantic image for the human condition, seen as clearly in the *Matrix* films as in romantic poetry, which assigns the distinctiveness of the human to the realm of 'feeling', as its weakness but usually also, at the end of the day, as its strength. What is very strange about this metaphor is its apparent reliance on some myth of empathy or telepathy.

I use the word 'telepathy' here deliberately, because it is the substance of an important book by Nicholas Royle, *Telepathy and Literature: Essays on the Reading Mind* (1990), and also of a chapter, 'The "Telepathy Effect"', in his more recent book, *The Uncanny* (2003). Part of this latter consists of a polemic against the uncritical use in supposedly critical thinking of the term 'omniscient' to describe certain kinds of narrator, a usage which has a lengthy history in Western criticism. This notion of omniscience, Royle suggests, is itself a metaphor, and a thoroughly motivated one in that it resides within the Judaeo-Christian tradition and essentially suggests a comparison between the role of the narrator and the role of God:

> Omniscience is not simply a hyperbole, it is an incoherent and flawed plot-device in a story that critics and theorists have been telling for a hundred years and more. Why retain the concept of omniscience at all? The use of the words 'omniscient' and 'omniscience' in the context of narrative fiction remains inextricably entangled in Christian motifs, assumptions and beliefs. To assume the efficacy and appropriateness of discussing literary works in terms of 'omniscient narration' is, however faintly or discreetly, to subscribe to a religious (and above all, a Christian) discourse and thinking.
>
> (Royle 2003: 260)

The narrator cannot know everything; strictly probed, this would reveal itself as an impossible supposition. It is doubly impossible, perhaps, because the writer of a certain kind of history may choose to claim omniscience on the grounds of knowing, and providing the knowledge of, all the facts, whereas what the writer of fiction knows about are, in the end, only his own creations; which, put like that, is hardly a remarkable, and certainly not a useful, view, despite the interesting take on it in John Fowles's *The French Lieutenant's Woman* (1969).

The reasons for Royle's preference for the term 'telepathy' – or, as he sometimes has it, 'clairvoyance' – are too long to explain fully here; but perhaps we might approach the topic through looking at one way in which a postmodern, or perhaps magic realist, novel, Rushdie's *Midnight's Children* (1981), foregrounds the telepathic properties of writer and text. Here a central plot device is that all the children born at the very moment of the partition of the Indian subcontinent, and thus at the birth of modern India, on 15 August 1947 are connected through a strange telepathy, which is also fully clairvoyant insofar as it enables the narrator, one such child, to see into the future, as he does, for example, in the closing paragraph of the novel:

> Yes, they will trample me underfoot, the numbers marching one two three, four hundred million five hundred six, reducing me to specks of voiceless dust, just as, all in good time, they will trample my son who is not my son, and his son who will not be his, and his who will not be his, until the thousand and first generation, until a thousand and one midnights have bestowed their terrible gifts and a thousand and one children have died, because it is the privilege and the curse of midnight's children to be both masters and victims of their times, to forsake privacy and be sucked into the annihilating whirlpool of the multitudes, and to be unable to live or die in peace.
>
> (Rushdie 1981: 463)

The narrator here is certainly claiming to see into the future; although it is interesting that the future also becomes in some sense metaphorical because some of that future has in fact already come to pass since the ostensible time of narration. And the metaphor strikes both ways, because the narrator foresees his own death, both as a person and as a narrator, at the same time as he is reduced to 'specks of voiceless dust'. What, though, is the massive act of telepathy for which *Midnight's Children* itself is a metaphor?

Presumably it is a metaphor for how subjectivity is not formed in isolation but rather in cultural, social and political contexts. We may not choose to believe literally that all children born at the same moment, however auspicious or menacing, have a kind of immediate radio contact; but at the same time, insofar as we are all 'children of our times', there will be links and connections between us which cannot be fully explained in terms of mere face-to-face contact. Here, this shared subjectivity is described in terms of a mixture of mastery and victimhood: one's understanding of the surrounding circumstances of the moment of one's own birth may afford one some purchase on the process of history, but at the same time it signifies the way in which we will be inexorably shaped by that history. The metaphor of the marching millions thus becomes both a metaphor for the tread of history and a kind of anti-metaphor for a myth of control: it is not we who are marching the march of history; rather, it is we who are that which will be obliterated by this onward march, which also in the context of this metaphor is a march that inevitably expands and increases as the population of India expands and increases.

Telepathy is thus here a metaphor, just as for Royle. It is a more satisfactory one than omniscience; but we might also go further and say that metaphor is itself in a certain sense telepathic, insofar as it asserts and affirms a common understanding among readers who may have no other physical or psychic proximity. We might go on (perhaps a little over-adventurously), though Royle does not himself go this far, to think of metaphor as ectoplasm: as the fruit of an attempt to give material form to, to incarnate, that which otherwise remains latent, ghostly. For metaphor, we may suggest, is not simply a matter of what appears on the printed page or in, for example, the work of visual art; it is rather the bodying-forth of sets of correspondences of which, in some sense, we have all, in specific interpretive communities, been aware in what we might define as a *liminal* way, hovering somewhere around the threshold of articulation.

Metaphor, then, can be seen as a kind or way of knowledge; but like all forms of knowledge it is not a knowledge *ab origine*, if such a thing can exist, but rather a concretisation, a constellation or reconstellation of that which has previously been held in private, which returns us to the metaphor of privacy in the Rushdie passage. At the most literal level, we might say that Rushdie is pointing to the way in which to have been born at a certain 'magical' moment forever robs us of our private life; more broadly, we might say that this very idea of privacy is itself a myth, a metaphor, because as we try to explain or understand another life we become automatically involved in a process of metaphorisation whereby we try to see the individual life as a metaphor for wider historical forces.

The phrase 'another life' might take us to the Caribbean writer Derek Walcott's 1973 volume of poetry published under that title. Chapter 1 of *Another Life* begins thus:

> Verandahs, where the pages of the sea
> are a book left open by an absent master
> in the middle of another life –
> I begin here again,
> begin until this ocean's
> a shut book, and like a bulb
> the white moon's filaments wane.
>
> (Walcott 1992: 145)

To begin this long poem with the word 'verandahs' is itself of interest, because the word has a lengthy and complex history. We are perhaps now inclined to think of it as an Indian word, since adopted into English; but in fact it is usually accepted that the Indian usage was itself a more distant import from a Spanish and older Portuguese word for 'railing, balustrade, balcony'. Thus, the word itself becomes a kind of master-metaphor for these issues of linguistic flux, and hence for the all-important issue for 'postcolonial' writers, which is the question of whose language one finds oneself using. If this is significant, then it acts in concert with the more extended metaphor of the 'pages of the sea', which at the same time implies something which is available to be 'read', as the interpretation of a convoluted past, as a purported explanation in this case of the predicament of West Indian cultures, while at the same time being perfectly unreadable. In this context, then, the metaphor of the 'absent master' opens in at least two directions. The 'absent master' may well be the writer of this delusively 'open book'; the phrasing here would also take us back to eighteenth-century Western notions of the *deus absconditus*, the absent deity who has set the universe in motion and then retired, as it were, behind the scenes. But the 'absent master', in the context of a culture rooted in slavery, would also remind the reader of precisely that history, of the plantation slave-master who profits at a distance from the labours of others. Thus, a dialectic of mastery and slavery is conjured into being, as one of the hidden stories; the sea does not really reveal this story, it has been erased, and here we are back again, perhaps, with 'lines drawn in the sand', but at the same time it has formed the ground, the ineradicable substrate, upon which West Indian consciousness is built.

In these contexts, the metaphor of 'another life' disseminates itself across a wide variety of discourses. An 'other' life would be the imagining of a life not already damaged by the history of transportation and slavery, by the sea's literal and metaphorical collusion in the terrors of the 'middle passage'. 'Another life' might also gesture towards the possibility of sur-passing, transcending these processes of historical damage by managing another kind of writing, the setting up of an alternative history. Or the 'other life' might refer directly to the life of the 'absent master', a life conducted in another place, beyond the range or comprehension of those whom he controls, and which is felt only in the imprint it leaves upon the pages of the lives of those descended from slave forebears. To 'begin . . . again' asserts the newness of this account, the account which the poet is going to deliver in the following 'pages', but at the same time asserts the impossibility of newness, of originality, when everything has already been 'stamped' with the mark of the 'absent master', like the branding of a slave.

There is, the passage seems to imply, the possibility of 'another life'; but perhaps not here and not now (as E.M. Forster put it in *A Passage to India* [1924]). The poem, therefore, cannot be or become what it states it wishes to become; it is already, from the beginning, dragged down by the weight of all that has passed, of all that is the past, and the struggle to form the new is inevitably already shaped by the metaphors by which we have come to live.

Here again, then, we have an image, a metaphor, of 'the text instead'. However, as well as these strenuous musings on otherness, on alterity, there is a further metaphorical resonance to 'another life'; this is, perhaps, *merely* 'another life', one of the unmarked, unremarkable lives of Rushdie's hundreds of thousands, of those who are bypassed, ignored by history. An early autobiographical text by a freed African slave is titled *The Interesting Narrative of the Life of Olaudah Equiano*, which was published in Britain in 1789. One might fairly ask why the word 'interesting' needs to be in that title: is it, perhaps, because otherwise the life of an ex-slave might indeed be deemed uninteresting? Is it indeed because the readership might have misgivings about the ability of an African to write a narrative, to give an account of himself, in any way that might be interesting to a white reader? The whole structure of Equiano's book is itself a kind of metaphor, because in it he both recounts his life as a slave and gives some account of the circumstances under which he obtained his freedom, and of what followed from that; but it is simultaneously, in a way which may remind us of the four levels of classical biblical interpretation, an account of his discovery of God, of his adoption of Christianity. We might then call this a narrative of redemption, which assumes a mythic or metaphorical structure taken over precisely from the culture of those masters whom Equiano is trying to evade; certainly, the potential story of Equiano *as an African* is progressively taken over, as the narrative develops, by the story of a Christian convert.

There is thus no pure narrative to be had here. Equiano's narrative, in a sense, *enacts what is expected of narrative*; it succumbs to a set of assumed narrative preoccupations, just as it is indeed difficult to write a diary in any kind of free form. When writing a diary, one inevitably writes in a form which accords with one's inner suppositions of what a diary is like, and thus the possibilities of imaginative freedom are simultaneously foreclosed by the 'unfreedom' of the dictates of a specific form; what is revealed is that, only too frequently, our metaphors are not our own. There would be strong comparisons here, which might be pursued, with J.M. Coetzee's dealings with history and narrative in *Waiting for the Barbarians* (1980), which has its own highly specific take on the postcolonial.

5

METAPHOR AND PSYCHOANALYSIS

In the fantasy novelist Terry Pratchett's *Guards! Guards!* (1989) there is a character called Carrot. Despite being self-evidently human, he has been brought up as a dwarf, despite being six foot five, and is understandably confused as to his nature. He joins the City Watch, and writes home to his mother:

> Last night the dragon burned up our Headquarters and Lo and Behold we have been given a better one, it is in a place called Pseudopolis Yard, opposite the Opera House. Sgt Colon says we have gone Up in the World . . . Going Up in the World is a metaphor, which I am learning about, it is like Lying but more decorative.
>
> (Pratchett 1989: 183)

In a way this returns us to older arguments mentioned above about the role of metaphor as decorative or constitutive; but the point here is that in Pratchett's fantasy realm of Discworld the dwarves themselves are a metaphor, not for the first time in literary and folk traditions, for a certain literality. Because of this accident of upbringing, or so we are led to suppose, Carrot does not have an innate understanding of metaphor; it seems to him to be a peculiar habit, and it takes him a great deal of effort to get his mind round it.

My point in using this example is to suggest that although it is customary to treat metaphor as a literary or rhetorical topic, it also and crucially has a psychological dimension. One of the enduring attempts to characterise psychotic thinking is that it is 'concrete' thinking; it manifests a state of mind (although it may not be continual since current thinking about psychosis has moved far more towards the idea that in most cases psychosis is 'episodic' rather than chronic) in which things are simply, and exactly, what they are. In this mindset there is no room for metaphor; to say that one thing is another thing is akin to lying. It follows that since such lying may be perceived under psychotic conditions as volitional on the part of the liar, persons who, or speech acts which, use metaphor may be perceived as wilful deceivers or deceptions. And from this origin a great deal can be concluded about the nature of, for example, paranoia, which can be characterised as a state of mind in which it appears as though lies are being perpetrated all the time, with the subject as the intended victim.

Another interesting feature of this *topos* in Pratchett's novel is that it is the dwarves who are the bearers of this concrete thinking. There are obviously numerous metaphorical extensions here, with dwarves being perceived in Western mythology up to J.R.R. Tolkien as those who toil against the 'bedrock' of experience, in mines and so forth; and dwarves are, by definition, though with the exception of Carrot, small, and their smallness might reasonably remind us of the state of childhood. The story of Snow White and the Seven Dwarves places us in a realm where Snow White is relegated to a kind of childhood; the pornographic and violent 1967 version of this story by the American writer Donald Barthelme goes further than this in speculating as to whether the dwarves' apparent innocence or ignorance is in fact itself a deception. However, it might be supposed that small children are themselves 'concrete thinkers', that the knowledge and understanding of metaphor is a later, superimposed development, but here we would run up against a problem.

This is that it appears that very small children are in fact adept natural users of metaphor; it seems as though this ability to practise and enjoy the mysterious equivalences between words and between things, present at very early stages, is temporarily lost at a certain stage of child development, possibly as an accompaniment to or effect of pre-pubertal anxiety. It is regained only later, perhaps then as a superimposition, as an always failing attempt to recapture the innocent metaphors of childhood play and make-believe. At stake here, indeed, is a whole question of belief. When a small child plays with, let us say, a teddy bear or a doll and has those objects construct or reconstruct a set of human interchanges, does the child in some sense 'believe' that these objects have some internal life of their own? Probably the question is unanswerable; but it is certain that in this example, as in the case of using a pencil, say, as a gun, some kind of metaphorical activity, which perhaps cannot be wholly reduced to Freudian versions of the phallus, is at stake. Perhaps all play is metaphor; perhaps all metaphor is play.

Certainly metaphor is in some sense the opposite of concrete thinking; and equally certainly the loss of the ability to think metaphorically renders the adult human subject severely dysfunctional. There are barely any words that can be uttered which will not carry and invoke a metaphorical dimension, and which might not thus suggest to the concrete thinker that a code is being employed to which he or she is not party, and which might therefore be considered to be oppressive, 'foreign', unavailable to meaningful translation.

To return to Pratchett's *Guards! Guards!* for a moment: towards the end of the book the major villain, a private secretary with the metaphorical name Lupine Wonse, is apprehended in a partially destroyed house by the forces of law and order under the command of the officer Vimes, but unwisely Wonse chooses to resist.

> Vimes shrugged. 'That's it, then,' he said, and turned away. 'Throw the book at him, Carrot.'
>
> 'Right, sir.'
>
> Vimes remembered too late.
>
> Dwarfs have trouble with metaphors.
>
> They also have a very good aim.
>
> *The Laws and Ordinances of Ankh and Morpork* caught the secretary on the forehead. He blinked, staggered, and stepped backwards.
>
> It was the longest step he ever took. For one thing, it lasted the rest of his life. After several seconds they heard him hit, five storeys below.
>
> (Pratchett 1989: 388)

The consequences, then, of taking metaphor literally can be deadly, and perhaps not only in a comic sense. Somewhat later, one of the novel's policemen opines, 'Killed by a wossname. A metaphor.' His companion replies, 'Dunno. Looks like the ground to me.' It may indeed seem merely comical to prefix the concept of the metaphor by the word 'wossname', but when we think about it, it becomes a most apt metaphor for metaphor. What, indeed, *is* its name? Perhaps metaphor begins when we find that experiences, however important or trivial, in truth do not have a name in any simple sense; according to this view, metaphor would be a continual process of trying to find names for things which in fact do not have names, trying to establish by analogy what it is that we are talking about when we talk to each other. As T.S. Eliot says, 'I gotta use words when I talk to you' (Eliot 1963: 135), and using words inevitably entails using metaphors.

I want now to turn more directly to psychoanalytical thinking, and also at least implicitly to its more recent linguistically oriented variants, as in, particularly, the French psychoanalyst Jacques Lacan as he elaborated on Freud. Lacan installed metaphor alongside metonymy as the central effects of the psychic processes of condensation and displacement, thus continuing with the process of turning metaphor from the status of a device or peculiarity of language towards a reflection of the wider ways in which humans consciously or unconsciously deal with the world. The evolution of a language, according to these ideas, can no longer be treated separately from the formation of subjectivity, and metaphor comes to be seen as an essential factor in the psychic apprehension of outer and inner worlds. Thus, metaphor becomes the primary feature in a *lecture symptomale* according to which reading and diagnosis become ineluctably linked as modes of interpretation.

I will not here go into the plethora of ways in which the terms 'metaphor' and 'metonymy' may be distinguished; instead, I will suggest some ways in which one of the primary processes which psychoanalysis claims to discern, the process of dream, displays a metaphorical structure, or in other words a structure within which one thing stands for another; which is, according to Freud, the basis of all dream.

Let us consider one of the many dream-situations to which Freud attends in his master-work, *The Interpretation of Dreams* (1900).

All the dreams of one of my women patients were characterized by her being 'rushed': she would be in a violent rush to get somewhere in time not to miss a train, and so on. In one dream *she was going to call on a woman friend; her mother told her to take a cab and not to walk; but she ran instead and kept on falling down.* – The material which came up in analysis led to memories of rushing about and romping as a child. One particular dream recalled the favourite children's game of saying a sentence '*Die Kuh rannte, bis sie fiel*' ['The cow ran till it fell'] so quickly that it sounds as though it were a single [nonsensical] word – another *rush* in fact. All these innocent rushings-about with little girl friends were remembered because they took the place of other, less innocent ones.

(Freud 1958: 199)

As so often with Freud, it is not easy to know exactly what he means when he speaks of the 'less innocent', although it may not be difficult to guess that he is delicately alluding to sexual content. The main point, however, is that these dreams are seen as unfolding themselves through a series of metaphorical reconstructions. The 'rushing', the haste, perhaps even the 'being rushed', all signify in some sense the romping of the child; what Freud does not say, but surely implies, is that the fact that these metaphors emerge only in the context of the dream, or in other words as an aspect of otherwise repressed material, must in some way relate to a difficulty to be found in relation to this childhood romping, whether this difficulty be located in the patient's own repressions or in the attitudes taken by the adult world towards her attempts at self-expression. Indeed, from a psychoanalytic point of view, those two aetiologies could hardly be clearly distinguished.

The example of the children's game is equally interesting, because Freud here seems to be pointing towards a kind of equivalence between what we might call life habits and linguistic habits. What might it mean when we 'rush our words'? And this touches upon another major Freudian theme, that of parapraxis or the slip of the tongue, which, in a way, is one of the most significant of Freud's contributions to literary criticism. To put it very crudely: what does it *mean* when we say, 'That is not what I meant'?

We might turn to Eliot, and to a typically convoluted passage from 'The Love Song of J. Alfred Prufrock' (1917):

And would it have been worth it, after all,
After the cups, the marmalade, the tea,

Among the porcelain, among some talk of you and me,
Would it have been worth while,
To have bitten off the matter with a smile,
To have squeezed the universe into a ball
To roll it towards some overwhelming question,
To say: 'I am Lazarus, come from the dead,
Come back to tell you all, I shall tell you all' –
If one, settling a pillow by her head,
    Should say: 'That is not what I meant at all:
    That is not it, at all'.

(Eliot 1963: 16)

To say, 'that is not what I meant' is a significant discursive and psychological move. If what one has said is not what one *meant* to say, then the question necessarily arises as to who it is that has said the thing that one did not mean to say. It is at this point that psychoanalysis arrives with an answer, which is that the subject who speaks is not a self-coherent, undivided subject in control of his or her own metaphorical structures; the subject who speaks is, in one sense, a puppet, at the mercy and under the authority of a different self within the self, an unconscious master who is speaking all the while, although we can perhaps attend to that other only in our dreams or on the analyst's couch.

The question of whether Freud's woman patient was, or became, aware of this complexity within her own metaphors of 'rushing' must remain forever imponderable, held in private or in secret. But the general idea that metaphorical structures of this kind, released through an uncanny combination of dream and the interpretation of dream, form a kind of base for what one might think of as less 'primitive' literary or narratological structures of metaphor remains as a necessary backdrop for our attempts to deal with the metaphorical. And in his analysis Freud is using, or suggesting, his own metaphors: we might speculate as to why it came to *his* mind, because there is no evidence that it came to the mind of his patient, that what was partially at stake here was a condition wherein language approaches a condition of nonsense.

The idea of nonsense is worth pursuing, if only because Lewis Carroll and Edward Lear – the two writers in the English tradition who are most concerned with some kind of definition of nonsense, if there can be such a thing – are also two writers about whom a great deal has been said from a psychoanalytical point of view. Let us consider whether, and in what sense, a poem in the mould of Lear can be a metaphor; while at the same time keeping psychoanalysis in the field as a mode of interpretation. A good example might be 'The Jumblies' (1871), of which this is the first stanza:

> They went to sea in a Sieve, they did,
>   In a Sieve they went to sea:
> In spite of all their friends could say,
> On a winter's morn, on a stormy day,
>   In a Sieve they went to sea!
> And when the Sieve turned round and round,
> And every one cried, 'You'll all be drowned!'
> They called aloud, 'Our Sieve ain't big,
> But we don't care a button! we don't care a fig!
>   In a Sieve we'll go to sea!'
>   Far and few, far and few,
>   Are the lands where the Jumblies live;
>   Their heads are green, and their hands are blue,
>   And they went to sea in a Sieve.

> (Lear 1947: 71)

This type of poem of Lear's is a parody; in particular, it is a parody of the type of sonority which we might expect of mainstream Victorian poetry, and perhaps particularly of the poetry of Alfred Lord Tennyson. Nevertheless, one might also pick up in this stanza a specific use of metaphor, but one which is strangely displaced; it would be, as it were, a metaphor for the apparently meaningless, for the prospect of an absurd rejection of supposedly conventional human norms. But in psychoanalytic terms, this might again throw us back on the question of what dreams may be metaphors for, of how we fulfil desires which we do not consciously know we have on the screen, or in the territory, of the ridiculous.

This type of metaphor might be termed a *metaphor towards nowhere*. The idea of the journey has been, since earliest times, perceived as a metaphor for human life; but in this poem this comfortable accepted metaphor is overturned. The sieve may indeed be seen as a metaphor for the instability and precariousness of human life; but it may also be seen as a metaphor for that uncertain world of dream and the unconscious where there is a total absence of stability, where there is no certainty or security of containment, where at any moment everything might be spilt or leaked. There is a whole theory of psychoanalysis, to be found particularly in the work of the French analyst Didier Anzieu, which bases itself in the notion of the container or envelope. This notion further bases itself in the notion that the work done by the ego, the conscious self that patrols the absurd desires of the unconscious, is designed to contain, to provide an apparently stable envelope for contents that might otherwise be spilt or contaminated. Here, what Lear appears to be doing is conjuring up that world in which such prospects of security or containment are unavailable: a more primitive world where we are not shielded from risk, and where we are not sure where suitable boundaries might be.

If, then, many conventional uses of metaphor seem designed to persuade us that 'X is like Y', what we have here is a use of metaphor that may open us to the possibility that, in fact, there is no real 'likeness' to be found: that the world in which such likenesses may be established is itself unspeakably precarious; that the metaphor of the sieve may be more appropriate to a childlike state in which we are, or have been, uncertain of our own boundaries, at the mercy of the 'stormy day'. This exposes us to the notion that a stable meaning for the term and process of metaphor itself may be at the mercy of wider forces, and of what it might be like to be in a world where metaphor is not possible or, at least, not credible.

It could also be said that Lear's limericks, for which he is best known, are in themselves resolute attempts at a denial of metaphorical extension. A common misapprehension of the limerick form is that it succeeds, with more or less difficulty, in finding three rhyming terms for the ends of the three long lines (lines 1, 2 and 5). In fact, Lear's limericks almost never do this; instead, they deny the 'journey' of matching lines by returning in the fifth line to exactly the position and the rhyming word of the first line.

> There was an old man of Port Grigor
> Whose actions were noted for vigour;
>   He stood on his head
>   Till his waistcoat turned red,
> That eclectic old man of Port Grigor.
>
> (Lear 1947: 181)

And so at the end we return to the beginning with no apparent extension of meaning, with, as it were, no 'journey' accomplished; except that it may be worthwhile looking again at the word 'eclectic', which can be paralleled many times in Lear's limericks as one of a series of operative words in the final line (other examples would include 'anxious', 'lively', 'elastic', 'unpleasing', and so on). What this may suggest is that the individual limerick as a whole provides a kind of commentary on the meaning of that crucial word. Except that it rarely actually does:

> There was on old person of Pinner,
> As thin as a lath, if not thinner;
>   They dressed him in white,
>   And roll'd him up tight,
> That elastic old person of Pinner.
> (Lear 1947: 201)

It would be hard to say that anything metaphorical is gained by the deployment of the word 'elastic' in the final line, hard to say that the reader's senses and understanding are expanded by its mention. Yet, around this apparent and, it seems fair to say, entirely deliberate defeat of meaning, it may be that something coagulates. There is a sense, perhaps, of the limitations of metaphor, a sense of the nonsensicality of language when it is reduced to its constituent parts and equally or further reduced by the continuing nonsensicality of the parallelisms asserted by rhyme, which is in a sense a site of absolute randomness, a pure accident of etymological and phonological history.

Perhaps critical here is that a proper psychoanalytical approach to metaphor does not imply, as has sometimes seemed to be the case, any attempt to comprehend the author's psyche, since such a psyche is, obviously, forever beyond our reach. Instead, such an approach deals in the text itself, and what that text reveals as we address it and try to understand it. It also implies that metaphors are not always, if indeed ever, a matter of choice; it is not as though we go forward and pick or design our metaphors, but more that we live within a continuing metaphorical structure and, furthermore, within a structure which largely determines what it might mean to be metaphorical. Metaphor, in this sense, becomes something of a sliding scale, about which psychoanalysis has much to say;

as also does the seminal work by George Lakoff and Mark Johnson, *Metaphors We Live By* (1980).

We might consider, for example, the work of a thinker from a quite different stream of analytical thinking, the neo-Jungian analytical psychologist and writer on myth James Hillman. In *The Dream and the Underworld* (1979), he both picks up on notions of the difference of the unconscious and relates them to elements in Platonic thinking:

> According to Plato . . . dream images are comparable with shadows, 'when dark patches interrupt the light', leading us to see a kind of 'reflection', 'the reverse of the ordinary direct view'. This useful analogy presents dreams as dark spots, the lacunae or ab-senses of the dayworld, where the dayworld reverses itself or converts its sense to metaphorical significance. This is not merely the dayworld repeated in a thinner silhouette of two dimensions. Like any visual shadow, these images shade in life, giving it depth and *twi*-light, duplicity, metaphor. The scene in a dream (the root of the word scene is akin to *skia*, 'shadow') is a metaphorical version of that scene and those players of yesterday who have now deepened and entered my soul.
>
> (Hillman 1979: 54)

There are many points here that one could pick up, and especially in a discourse like Hillman's which is itself vastly metaphorical and at the same time aware of its own metaphoricity. Perhaps the most significant phrase is the one which claims that dreams are places 'where the dayworld reverses itself or converts its sense to metaphorical significance'. Thus, one might say, the dream can never be read literally, because its very substance is metaphor; but thus also one might claim that the point of dream, if there is such a thing, is continually to 're-mind' the subject that without metaphor the world makes no 'sense'. The act of dream in confronting us with what Hillman calls 'ab-sense' continually *undermines* our 'dayworld' sense that the world is as it is; it reminds us that we make sense of the world only by perceiving likenesses and differences between things and other things; thus, metaphor becomes itself a metaphor for the continuing encounter with the other which makes up most of our mental life.

Metaphor and dream do not then merely repeat the world in any clearly mimetic sense, any more than literature, poetry, the arts 'repeat' or represent the world. Rather, they put it through a series of changes, inversions, and even, especially in the case of dream, subject it to violent incongruities. But Hillman also goes further than this and compares the metaphorising activity of dream to a drama, a 'scene', and he refers particularly to the 'players of yesterday'. By this he means several things. First, he means to refer to a mythical or metaphorical past, whether that be best conceived in Freudian terms of ancient complexes deriving from primal Oedipal conflicts or in Jungian terms as the enactment of the archetypes. This long past, he claims, is re-enacted nightly, but in metaphorical, transferred form. Second, he means to refer to what Freud preferred to call the 'day's residues'. Freud meant this, perhaps, in a rather literal sense: that the materials from which our dreams are woven are frequently bits and pieces, scraps left over from the encounters with the other that we may have had, literally, on the preceding day. This is why sleep deprivation is so dangerous, and perhaps that is also because it robs us of the vitality of our stock of metaphor. But for Hillman, the 'day's residues' would be those parts of our dayworld experience which have not yet been subject to metaphorisation; and this would be why, no doubt to the frustration of all of us, the figures that appear in dream often appear to have a trivial aspect. The metaphors of dream serve to challenge and perhaps to correct that assignation of the trivial, to alert us to the fact that the only reason they have appeared trivial is because we have had neither the will nor the time to experience their own shadow, the work that would convert them into their own other aspect, according to which they would reveal their metaphorical potential.

Hillman's claim for metaphor, then, would be that it deepens our understanding; but for him, following the whole history of Western myth, deepening also implies darkening. He often says that the most significant, all-encompassing thing about dream is that it takes place in a darkened world. Thus, metaphor, too, would be something of the dark, something never fully revealed to, or interpreted by, the full light (to use the conventional metaphor) of the understanding. We strive to understand metaphor; that is part of our task as readers, as students of literature, indeed as human beings, because without that attempt at understanding we would be lost in the psychotic; but we can never fully arrive at a resolution, because metaphors have something in common with, for example, the paintings of M.C. Escher, or with the Rorschach blot, both of which are famously indecipherable or, at least, irreducible to a single interpretation: they can never fully reveal their own meanings because they are perennially on the point of turning into their own other.

Let us consider a specific example of Hillman's approach to the metaphorical function. Here, he is writing about the classical myth of Hercules' journey to Hades:

> Hercules had to go mad, literally, in order to understand the underside of things, maybe because his journey to Hades was a mess. When imagining Hercules in the House of Hades . . . – his aggressiveness in drawing his sword, aiming his arrow, wounding Hades in the shoulder, slaughtering cattle, wrestling the herdsman, choking and chaining Cerberos – we are presented with the imaginal paradigm of the life instinct, as Freud called it, within the realm of the death instinct . . . This fusion is precisely, according to Freud, the origin of aggressivity . . . Rather than *die to metaphor* [my italics], we kill literally; refusing the need to die, we attack death itself. Our civilization, with its heroic monuments, tributes to victory over death, ennobles the Herculean ego, who does not know how to behave in the underworld.
>
> (Hillman 1979: 110)

The root of what Hillman is saying here is that the origin of the violent, aggressive self, which is summarised in the labours of Hercules, lies in a misunderstanding about the metaphorical nature of the world. Instead of understanding death or Hades as part of his own make-up or destiny, Hercules represents a mode of action which instead seeks to externalise death and vanquish it in the form of a perceived enemy. It would be difficult to miss the comparisons Hillman is drawing through his allusions to, for example, 'heroic monuments' with the roots of militaristic behaviour, the lust for occupation and conquest, which have been a hallmark of so-called civilisation down the centuries.

What Hercules, and thus the Herculean part of the ego, cannot or will not understand is that he is, to use the Quixotic phrase, 'tilting at windmills': the enemies he imagines are there only because he is not able to inspect his own inner world and its rich stock of metaphor for life and death. What would it mean, then, in Hillman's challenging and puzzling phrase, to 'die to metaphor'? Well, it would clearly not mean to die 'in' metaphor, or in other words to accept all metaphors for death into one-self, to retract from the world and cease to engage with complexities of aggressivity and the other. But it might mean to perform a certain act of surrender to metaphor, to understand and to face the fact – as Hercules, among many other 'heroes', appears unable to do – that life's difficulties cannot be understood by translating them into the literal; that we have to understand that the 'shadow of metaphor' is just as present to us as the dayworld; that without this process we are condemned to living in a one-dimensional world.

For Hillman, then, metaphor represents a deepening, an intensification of the world in which we customarily think we live. Analytical psychology, the Jungian version of psychoanalysis, claims to be able to help this process by enabling us to relate our dreams and experiences to a metaphorical backdrop, without which we would be reduced to a series of unrelated events and phenomena; metaphor is the way in which we bind things together. These things can be bound together in helpful ways which will improve our understanding; but they can also be bound together in unhelpful ways, as when we succumb to the all-pervasive shallow stereotyping of the tabloid press. But the point is that there is no third alternative; it appears, according to Hillman, to be the case that this metaphorical process is inexorably imbricated with our relations to the other; it is not something we can stand outside.

We could take this further by looking at a book by the contemporary Scottish novelist Iain Banks, *The Bridge* (1986). This is a complex novel which works on many levels. At the heart of it is a man, interestingly and ambiguously named Orr, who has suffered a near-fatal car accident, and the whole novel, although we do not know this until the end, takes place during his subsequent coma. In the course of this coma his psyche is split into several parts, and so the novel consists of several different, interlaced narratives, some apparently more 'realistic' than others.

The most relevant for our purposes, however, is the narrative told by a figure known only as the Barbarian. He speaks, or rather the novel linguistically represents him as speaking, with a strong, at times nearly impenetrable, Glaswegian accent, very different indeed from the compara-tively unmarked English of the other parts of the narrative of this shattered psyche. One could say that this discourse represents the unconscious; but it also relates closely to Hillman's ideas on metaphor, and especially to his comments (outlined above) on the mythic figure of Hercules as an emblem of 'resistance to metaphor'. For it is clear that the world the Barbarian finds himself inhabiting is the world of Greek myth: he encounters Cerberos and Charon; he finds himself freeing various captive maidens, though not before conveniently raping them; but he does all this in apparently total ignorance of the story, of the series of metaphors, which he is inhabiting.

The Barbarian – a name which is extremely well chosen – thus represents that part of the self which does not know, or prefers not to know, what part of the story, or what kind of story, he is enacting; his actions represent the kinds of action we might find ourselves undertaking if we were unaware of the complexity of metaphor. It is interesting that he is accompanied on his violent adventures by a figure known only as the 'familiar', who sits on his shoulder, speaks perfect received-pronunciation English, and occasionally tries to tell the Barbarian the folly of his ways. But he does so only in an ironic, even cynical tone; he is aware, as we readers are aware, that his words will not change the Barbarian's course of action; the Barbarian is programmed to kill, torture and maim, to act purely on the literalistic demands of the unconscious; he is immune to the demands of the civilised, and cannot see himself as part of any greater mythic world than the one in which he thinks he has been placed to carry out primal struggles and gratify his primal and extremely violent desires.

If we accept that the distinction between the unconscious and the ego is a distinction between barbaric and civilised behaviour, contentious as such a claim may still remain, then what *The Bridge* shows us is that this is also a question of metaphor. The language the Barbarian speaks is a brutalised language; it is devoid of complexity, it addresses primitive needs and satisfactions head-on. What is perhaps most significant is that it is thus in some sense doomed to failure, as in the case of Hercules' madness; it is not possible to make sense of the world without a sense of metaphor, without a sense of the inverse which always shadows our searchings.

Any number of Western stories have told and retold this truth, from the fourteenth-century poem *Sir Gawain and the Green Knight* to 'Childe Roland to the Dark Tower came'. The essential structure of myths and stories like these is that the hero arrives at a point, or in a place, where his own writ does not run: he finds himself at the mercy of a different and complex power which typically, like the Oracle or the Sibyl in ancient

Greece, appears to have greater authority than he has. His task then becomes not simply to free the maiden or kill the monster, but to understand the deeper, metaphorical truth which is being offered; to try to comprehend the underlying purpose of his quest. Perhaps the most enduring emblem of this structure in British literature has been the quest for the Holy Grail. One might argue that the Grail is a chalice, with connections to the death of Christ; or that it is a symbol for an unending quest, wherein truth, whatever that may be, continually eludes us; or that it is a *rite de passage*, whereby the significance of the myth has little to do with the Grail itself but rather with the various tests which the questors have to pass or fail. What may, however, be an even more deeply underlying truth is that the Grail *is*, in some sense, metaphor itself; it marks the point at which literal truth, the possibility of complete success or understanding, forever vanishes, where the apparently enlightened truths of life give way to a certain darkness, a darkness within which, according to the legend, the Grail continues to shine, but within which also it may remain forever ungraspable, forever out of reach in the darkened world which we try to reach but also fear entering.

6

METAPHOR, THE
UNCANNY, *DÉJÀ-VU*

In view of what we have said so far, what, we might ask, would be the more uncanny: to see the thing, the object, only in terms of what it is; or to see it in terms of what it is not, its identity as formed by the other? Metaphor is a crucial way in which we can apprehend the quality of the uncanny, considered as the process which establishes the inseparability of the familiar and the unfamiliar. To say that something is like something else is already to establish complex hierarchies of understanding; it is also to establish that in order to *recognise* something we have to 'see it again'. Thus, metaphor needs to be seen in terms of operations of power, by which something is recapitulated into recognisable terms; at the same time, this operation of recapitulation can never be complete because it falls under the sign of repetition, which points back towards the limit and incompletion of coherent subjectivity and threatens us with the possibility of uncomprehended returns. My concern here will be to make Freud's thinking clear on topics such as the uncanny and repetition, through the use of examples.

We have seen that one of the classic, and indeed classical, approaches to metaphor is to view it as a device or process whereby we can perceive the likeness of something to something else; the political State, we say, or perhaps said more frequently in Elizabethan times, is a body, a body 'politic'. And why, or in what sense, is it a body? Because it is 'like' a body, it resembles a body in particular respects, for example because every part of it is organically connected to every other part; because it has a head or chief part, which in some sense corresponds to the Head of State; because its collective well-being benefits every part of it; and so on.

But this question of likeness is perhaps not as easy as it sounds. For if any one thing can be like any one other thing, there can and must be between those things also a difference; otherwise, they would be exactly the same thing, and any available metaphor would collapse into identicality. Metaphor, therefore, asserts both similarity and difference. It might say that, on the one hand, we can apprehend life as a circle, as in many religious doctrines, but at the same time we become hauntingly aware that there are also many ways in which life is not a circle: we are not, for example, the same at the end of it as we were at the beginning.

It is on this basis that I want to attend to some ways in which this dialectic of similarity and difference might remind us of the collection of experiences and factors which we refer to under the heading 'the uncanny'. The uncanny received its first serious and complex description by Freud in his short text 'The "Uncanny"' in 1919. Here, Freud begins by pointing to a peculiarity in the German word '*unheimlich*', which could be literally translated as 'unhomely' (Freud 1955: 220). But, says Freud, the word '*unheimlich*' has come through linguistic history to encompass also its own opposite. It signifies the 'unhomely' in the sense of that which is strange, unusual, perhaps even inexplicable; but it also signifies that which is very much 'at home', in the sense of that which is held as secret, intimate, unrevealed. The province of the uncanny, then, is not merely that which is strange, weird, perhaps even frightening; what is uncanny is that which, although it may seem unusual and out of the ordinary, in some sense also reminds us of something that has 'gone before'. Thus, the uncanny is intimately bound up with a notion of repetition, but of repetition with a difference: 'the uncanny', Freud says, 'is that class of the frightening which leads back to what is known of old and long familiar' (Freud 1955: 220).

In this light we might consider, for example, a short poem by Thomas Hardy, 'Lying Awake' (1927):

You, Morningtide Star, now are steady-eyed, over the east,
    I know it as if I saw you;
You, Beeches, engrave on the sky your thin twigs, even the least;
    Had I paper and pencil I'd draw you.

You, Meadow, are white with your counterpane cover of dew,
    I see it as if I were there;
You, Churchyard, are lightening faint from the shade of the yew,
    The names creeping out everywhere.

                         (Hardy 2001: 863)

There are many things one could say about this dense and exquisite poem. My main point, however, is to describe it as an evocation of the haunting, uncanny power of metaphor. For one of the crucial features of the narrative position in the poem is that the narrator, wherever he might be (if it is a 'he'), and indeed whether he is even alive, is crucially *not there*: he is not, he claims, in a position to see the 'Morningtide Star', nor to draw the beeches, nor to appreciate the beauty of the whitened meadow, nor to apprehend the slow dawn of colour in the churchyard.

Yet, while he is 'not there', and although we as readers do not know where he is, nevertheless precisely the phenomena which in one breath he claims to be unable to observe he is simultaneously conveying to us as readers by his representation of them. All of the images of the poem are in some sense metaphors for life, or at the very least for survival: the 'thin twigs' of the beech trees, for example. The narrator is in some sense 'at home' with them, in that he can use them as relatively common objects that can serve as vehicles for communication between himself and his readers; even though in another sense he is utterly estranged from them. They are *unheimlich* to him, between him and them there appears to be an insurmountable barrier, a barrier which, as I have implied (and which might be further brought out by the prominent positioning of the names of the graves), might perfectly well be the barrier of death.

We are thus, as readers, in the uncanny position of being addressed by a voice which, on the one hand, appears to come from nowhere, even perhaps from the world of death itself, while at the same time it speaks to us, metaphorically, in the most ordinary of manners from the page. And the way in which this distance is gauged and negotiated is precisely through the use of metaphor; through the use of normal, *heimlich* objects like beech trees, meadows, even, at another level of metaphor, bedclothes, in order to bring an otherwise incomprehensible world within the domain of the intelligible. As Freud resonantly put it in another context, analogies may decide nothing, but they have the capacity for making one feel more at home (Freud 1960: 210–11).

Having said that, however, one could immediately return to Hardy's poem and ask whether, in the end, the metaphors *do* make the reader feel 'more at home'. One might alternatively say that the insistence on the unavailability of the beech trees, their distance from whatever state or condition we imagine the protagonist to be inhabiting – be it death, sickness or depression, to name the most likely candidates – serves rather to sharpen or heighten our sense of the *unheimlich*, of *not* being at home; of, perhaps, never being able to feel convincingly at home again. The metaphors are both vivid and, in the context of the narrator's perspective upon them, impossible to grasp; as such, they represent something of the general nature of representation, which on the one hand grips us with the utmost immediacy and, on the other, constantly reminds us that the objects or emotions being represented are, above all, *not there*; that they, and therefore also we as readers, are far from home.

One of the best-known forms, and some would say the emblematic form, of the uncanny is *déjà-vu*. Now, in one sense *déjà-vu* might seem a simple concept, and to mean, exactly as in French, that which is 'already seen'. But the more we think about this formulation, the less satisfactory it seems. After all, we all spend our time seeing things we have already seen; our own homes, the neighbouring streets, our loved ones, and so forth. Although hardly without interest, one could nevertheless not say that these experiences are uncanny, and certainly they do not amount to *déjà-vu*; otherwise, whenever we saw our pet cat we would be struck with amazement and uncertainty, one probable result of which is that the unfortunate cat would starve. When we say that we have experienced *déjà-vu* we are trying to describe, possibly hopelessly, a much more disturbing experience. Probably no words *can* fully describe it; but one attempt would be to say that it is an experience in which we feel an uncanny *resemblance*, an inexplicable matching between present and past which momentarily destabilises our sense of linear time; we have an experience of an uncanny matching between two discrete events, or occurrences, a matching which *should not* have occurred. Something unnatural has happened.

There is, we might fairly contend, something similarly unnatural about metaphor. In a meeting which I recently attended, one of the participants, attempting to describe a scheme for incentivising his colleagues and producing more and harder work from them, declared that there should at all costs be 'a carrot at the end of the tunnel'. Now, the first thing one would want to say about this is that it is, in the sense we have mentioned before, a mixed metaphor: that is, there is an evident disjunction between its parts, which in this case is rendered particularly clear by the fact that it mixes two deeply rooted metaphors, 'a light at the end of the tunnel' and 'the carrot and the stick'. But it is possible to think further into this, because one can see something almost magically metaphorical about this mixed metaphor, although in order to do so one would need to, as it were, change one's subject position; one might need, for example, to become a rabbit, or possibly a rabbit–mole hybrid. There could, I would argue, be a strange flash of recognition here, something akin to *déjà-vu* in one particular way; namely, in the way in which metaphor, the uncanny and *déjà-vu* all collect around the notion of dream.

Consider, for example, Franz Kafka's famous story 'Metamorphosis' (1915), in which the protagonist, as the story begins, awakes to find that he has been transformed into a giant cockroach. Now, we are clearly unlikely to be satisfied as readers with the thought that this transformation has actually occurred, whatever that may mean; and one of the first things we will do, as we would if somebody we were talking to suddenly declared, 'I am a donkey,' is to search for a convenient metaphorical meaning, some kind of structure which will enable us to make sense of the text in terms of a kind of one-to-one equivalence. In the case of the man who declares himself a donkey, we might wish to enquire which of the donkey's legendary propensities he considers himself to possess: excessive stupidity, very long ears, remarkable sexual prowess, or indeed all of these. In the case of a literary text like 'Metamorphosis', or indeed of any other written text, we cannot ask this question and so we are thrown further back on our own imaginative resources. (Another well-known example of this kind of process, incidentally, would be Eugène Ionesco's 'absurdist' play *Rhinoceros* (1958), also a tale of translation or metamorphosis.)

However, it would seem fair to say that if were to settle upon any *specific* metaphorical reading of Kafka's text, or a meaning for what we might term 'the cockroachness of it all', then we would be in some sense undervaluing the text. We would be performing what I would call a *recuperative* reading. For one of the facts about metaphor is that it is *strange*. It cannot be simply recuperated by saying, 'Well, this is obviously like that', and therefore implying, without any lingering, haunting sense of strangeness, that this *is* that; there is always something left over in metaphor, something unaccountable, something that might make one feel that these equivalences might make sense in a dream but that in real life, whatever that may be, there has to be difference along with the similarity, some admixture of the unhomely with the homely.

Consider the famous phrases at the end of Orson Welles's classic film *Citizen Kane* (1941):

> Charles Foster Kane was a man who got everything he wanted, and then lost it. Maybe Rosebud was something he couldn't get or something he lost, but it wouldn't have explained anything. I don't think any word explains a man's life. No – I guess Rosebud is just a piece in a jigsaw puzzle – a missing piece.
>
> (Kael 1971: 294)

The film itself goes part of the way to explaining what Rosebud was. But it can never go the whole of the way because, as well as being a physical object, Rosebud is also a metaphor, just as is explained here, for something wider, broader, more indeterminate. It is a dream object, or an object seen under conditions of *déjà-vu*; it cannot be fully comprehended or grasped, but remains forever slightly out of reach. This is perhaps something of the sense which the Scottish/Cornish poet W.S. Graham is also trying to express when he says:

Enough

> Voices are here with me here and more
> The further I go. Yesterday
> I heard the telephone ringing deep
> Down in a blue crevasse.
> I did not answer it and could
> Hardly bear to pass.
>
> (Graham 2004: 154)

This poem is one of many of Graham's which seem to be set on an Arctic or Antarctic journey, where things become increasingly uncertain and unclear as he proceeds. But at the same time, it is evident from this and many other passages that this journey is also the journey into language which the poet undertakes as he or she begins to write. There are many metaphors which have been used to illuminate the poetic experience: some, especially since the romantic period, have involved a certain notion of 'finding oneself' or at least of 'finding one's own voice'. Graham's central metaphor for the poetic adventure is the reverse: it involves the constant risk of being lost, of carrying on even though there is no light at the end of the road, no carrot at the end of the tunnel, and even though one is entirely uncertain of one's direction or bearings, one has little choice but to press on. The uncanniness here, then, lies in the 'voices'; it is as though the poet, lost in his own strange journey, can nevertheless still hear the voices, the calls of the apparently normal, but for him they are transfigured; they themselves need to be metaphorised into his own landscape. And this is one common feature of dream: when in a dream you hear the noise of an approaching army coming over a hill, experience a moment of terrible panic, and wake to find that the alarm clock is shrilling, you are engaging, unconsciously of course, in a metaphorical process, translating one thing into another, seeking understanding through comparison.

To see another aspect of metaphor and the uncanny, we may turn to a wonderful sonnet of Tennyson's, usually known as 'Now Sleeps the Crimson Petal' (*c.* 1849):

> Now sleeps the crimson petal, now the white;
> Nor waves the cypress in the palace walk;
> Nor winks the gold fin in the porphyry font.
> The firefly wakens. Waken thou with me.
>
> Now droops the milk-white peacock like a ghost,
> And like a ghost she glimmers on to me.
>
> Now lies the earth all Danaë to the stars,
> And all thy heart lies open unto me.
>
> Now slides the silent meteor on, and leaves
> A shining furrow, as thy thoughts in me.

> Now folds the lily all her sweetness up,
> And slips into the bosom of the lake.
> So fold thyself, my dearest, thou, and slip
> Into my bosom and be lost in me.
>
> (Tennyson 1969: 318–19)

In one crucial sense this poem is similar to Hardy's, in that it invokes a powerful sense of *what is not there*; but it goes farther than Hardy's in its metaphorical structure. It is, as with Hardy's, a structure of negatives: the flower with the petals, the cypress, the goldfish, all these are 'no longer visible'; for the poet to conjure them is both a paradox and a kind of display of power, an uncanny power which is the hallmark of the poem.

Perhaps the most crucial line is 'And like a ghost she glimmers on to me'. What this seems to be is, at least in part, a metaphor for the poetic process: the peacock itself may be absent, or present but unseen to conventional eyes; but the poet, the metaphor seems to imply, has a special kind of perception to which the peacock continues to present itself in spectral form. Thus, the metaphors combine to establish a world of the ghostly: the peacock itself may be ghostly, but by a process of transferred epithet it becomes entirely possible that the poet himself is ghostly, is seeing as a phantom might see, and this contributes to the curious way in which here the imagery of love becomes strangely, indeed uncannily, menacing, as though the poet's ambition is not merely to embrace but entirely to enfold, obliterate, the other.

It is also worth noticing, as several critics have done, that there is a peculiar gender ambiguity at the heart of the metaphor. Unless the 'she' of the sixth line is itself transferred from the loved woman onto the peacock, which seems improbable since she is referred to in the second rather than the third person elsewhere in the poem, then we have a problem. The image 'peacock' conjures up is a miracle of colouring, which fits entirely with the uncanny interchange of colour and colourlessness elsewhere in the metaphorical structure of the poem; but a peacock is unmistakably male, as we are frequently reminded by other metaphorical usages of the peacock, as an image of 'strutting' and masculine display. As an aside, it may be that what the poet is thinking of is a peahen; but it is interesting in itself to consider what a bathetic effect would be produced in the poem were a peahen to be named as such, not to mention the fact that a peahen's colouring is entirely unremarkable.

I may appear to be labouring this point; but it does emphasise the power of the poet in this poem, whose implicit claim appears to be that by the sheer force of his language he can entice the loved one into an embrace which, to all purposes, appears to be potentially fatal, at least to her individuality. This is a ghost, a spectre, with real physical power, a frightening idea indeed. And this power is further underlined by the choice of the poem's location: far from suburban streets – those streets so ably and bleakly defined in another Tennyson poem, *In Memoriam* (1850) – this poem, this event, this memory, perhaps even this act of *déjà-vu*, takes place in a palace garden. All the metaphors, not only the peacock but also and perhaps most significantly the 'porphyry font', are metaphors informed by a certain *topos* of luxury and wealth.

If we were to trace this stream of metaphor further back, we might well come across an underlying mythic structure, as is the case with much metaphor. In this case, it could well again be the mythology of Hades or Pluto. According to this array of myths, the God of the Dead has many attributes, but one of them is the ability to confer immense wealth; this is whence we derive the word 'plutocracy'. This itself, one must presume, is an archaic metaphor for the power of death as well as the transience of mortal goods because material wealth is useless when you are dead. Yet again, there are other archaic versions of this: it may now be a cliché to say that 'you can't take it with you when you go', but this was presumably not apparent in ancient Egyptian culture, where status depended very largely on what *was* sent with you when you went, based on an assumption that this would ease your post-death passage through other worlds.

When thinking of the power of death, a further passage that might come to mind is a well-known one from James Elroy Flecker's 'The Old Ships' (1915):

> I have seen old ships sail like swans asleep
> Beyond the village which men still call Tyre,
> With leaden age o'ercargoed, dipping deep
> For Famagusta and the hidden sun
> That rings black Cyprus with a lake of fire.
>
> (Flecker 1916: 216)

One could say that there are various things that are uncanny about this passage. One is in the second line: 'which men still call Tyre'. If this is something that 'men' still do, then what exactly is the status of the narrator? Are we here in the company of a supernatural being? Whatever it is, its purpose seems to be at once to make the strange landscape portrayed more *and* less familiar to the reader; to bring us closer to the details of an ancient history while at the same time investing the scene with such peculiarities, such strange vividnesses, that it inevitably also distances us from it.

What has this to do with metaphor? One thing it might suggest is that the notion of the narrator is itself metaphorical. After all, there is no narrator here, in the sense of a being who is present to us telling us a story; there is only the discursive fiction of a narrator. Thus, the circles and coils of metaphor wind around narrative. To put it in a different context, who, to a child, is the narrator when having a story read? Is it the person reading, is it the author of the written story, if there has been one, or is it something else, perhaps a narrative function in the child's own mind which is continuously metaphorising, continuously turning the elements of the story to his/her own interests, into explanations or interpretations of puzzling facts and events in life?

There is a metaphor here of the most obvious type, a simile: 'like swans asleep'. But even here perhaps the words are more tricky than they seem. For the most obvious way of dealing with such a metaphor would be by saying that the sleeping swans are being compared to the old ships. But it could equally be argued that the sleeping swans are in fact a controlling metaphor or trope for the whole passage, insofar as they introduce the ideas of linked passivity and beauty, night-time and strength, which go on to determine the rest of the metaphorical structure of the piece.

There is also here, perhaps, an uncanniness of time. For in one sense it seems as though this somewhat Tiresias-like narrative figure is seeking to capture and present us with a large-scale historical scene; but in another he is presenting a particular moment, 'black Cyprus with a lake of fire', a specific scene at a particular moment of sunset. Thus, we are presented with the general and the specific tied together, which immediately suggests ambiguities, even paradoxes, about the key metaphor: are we meant to see here an enduring symbol of antiquity, or rather a fleeting sensation which can never be recaptured? Even to put this question is to enter the terrain

of *déjà-vu*, which, among other propensities, has the weird, uncanny quality of confusing us about how time moves, about the relation between
the moment and continuity, all the complications which the novelist
Russell Hoban (1962) refers to under the heading *The Moment under the
Moment*.

And there is the uncanny and the sense of metaphor even within a single
name: here, for example, Famagusta. It would obviously be possible to
identify what is evoked by the name 'Famagusta', but this would be too
simple an approach; it might be better to ask what 'Famagusta' metaphorically becomes in the context of this passage. It becomes a metaphor, a
symbol, for a certain notion of the Oriental, perhaps more specifically of
the Levantine. It becomes detached from its real location, if it has such
a thing, and enters into its own metaphorical field, and this is something
which happens with many ancient names, from Tyre and Sidon to Sodom
and Gomorrah. Part of the uncanniness in these names lies in the richness
of the metaphorical field they open up; we are naturally reminded that we
have heard these names before, that there is no possibility of 'innocence'
in regard to them, that any reading of them must necessarily invoke much
that has gone before in a half-unconscious realisation of repetition.

We might take this further by considering a short poem by Roy Fisher,
'The Wrong Time', which is part of a longer poem, *Interiors with Various
Figures* (1967):

> It's the wrong time; that makes it the wrong room:
> I'm here, he's not; he was here, he will be.
>
> Meanwhile, please use the place. It can use you,
> Your scent, silk, clean lines, mouthwash conversation.
> With him away it's sour and frowsty. You have
> To swell your light to absorb the faint bulb, scuffed greenish
>   walls, breakfast wreckage,
> Till the silk stitches hurt. You win. But the place contains me.
>
> I'm not what you want. You're not what I want. What do you
>   do with me?
> Do you take me in, with the milk in the bottom of the bottle;
>   dazzle me, with the grease spots, out of
>   reckoning?

> Or do you see round me, a man-shaped hole in the world?

> Looking at you, I can't tell. You don't seem to find it hard,
>   either way.

>   (Fisher 1980: 44–5)

We might begin to analyse the metaphorical structure of this poem by saying that the room is, among other things, a metaphor for a relationship. The objects perhaps within this room, the 'breakfast wreckage' and so forth, are also metaphors for a state of mind. But the question immediately arises, whose state of mind? This would take us into a consideration of the pronouns, of the pronominal structure of the poem, the 'I', the 'he', the 'you'. It would be simple to assume that there are direct relations between these 'persons', but in fact this becomes more complex and difficult to understand the longer one looks at the poem. It is perhaps no accident that Fisher uses the image of 'swelling light'; rather, as with efforts to look directly at bright light, there comes a point where all is, as Fisher puts it, 'dazzle', and individual figures are difficult to pick out.

This might refer us back to the overall title of the poem, *Interiors with Various Figures*. These 'interiors' are obviously, in one sense, rooms; but they are also the interiors of minds. Similarly, the figures are, in one sense, persons. But they may also be figures of speech: it is interesting that the phrase 'just a figure of speech' has become a cliché, as if for something to be a figure of speech in some way downgrades it. It may not be going too far to say that there is a certain denial going on in this view; that it is more convenient and comfortable to pretend that there are some speech forms which do not use figures of speech and thus give us access to a solid, incontrovertible perception of the real, in contrast to which the figure of speech is in some way abstracted, lacking in purchase.

We might say that a crucial figure of speech in this particular poem is apostrophe, which is helpfully defined by Martin Gray in his *Dictionary of Literary Terms* as 'a rhetorical term for a speech addressed to a person, idea, or thing' (Gray 1992: 31). He provides an amusing example from the Scottish poet Douglas Dunn's 'Ode to a Paperclip' (1981):

> When I speak to you, paperclip, urging you
> To get a move on and metamorphose,

You sit there mating with the light that shines
Out of your minerals, a brighter glint
Where, rounding at a loop, you meet the sun.
Paperclip, I like you, I need you.
Please, turn into something wonderful.
(Dunn 1986: 204)

Here the joke is on a whole tradition of poetry, perhaps especially the romantic ode, which chooses to address and thereby necessarily anthropomorphise non-sentient beings. But it is interesting to note that in the time since this poem was written in 1981 something 'wonderful', or at any rate strange, has indeed happened to the paperclip, namely its transformation into a virtual animate being in the form of Mr Clippy, the Word for Windows wizard symbol used by Microsoft and thus irritatingly familiar to so many of us. Thus, do metaphors move on, develop and sometimes, indeed, undercut themselves.

Also of interest is that Gray mentions at the beginning of his entry on apostrophe that the literal Greek meaning is 'turning away', but he does not go on to develop this idea, which is at first glance a strange, even an uncanny, one. How has it come to be that a word which originally meant 'turning away' has come down the centuries to signify direct address? There could be many answers to this question; one of them takes us back to the whole topic of address and of the pronominal structure of poetry. For if direct address to an object is a 'turning away', then what is turned away *from* is the reader; when reading an apostrophe we are both included in the poem and simultaneously excluded; we are no longer the direct recipient of the poem but are instead 'overhearing', to use a favourite term of the romantics, a dialogue or polylogue among others.

To turn back to Fisher's poem: we could say that what the reader is metaphorically hearing here is indeed a kind of conversation, but it is a conversation at many removes. We receive only its echoes, uncannily reaching us across many levels of uncertainty. Who, if anybody, after all, is actually 'here', 'in "the wrong room"'? Or are we overhearing a conversation between ghosts, or indeed only the voice of a single ghost, even if other voices seem also to be ringing inside his head? The crucial metaphors of hearing and looking are everywhere here, but they are also constantly threatening to break their bounds, to expose us to more than the eye can see or than the ear can hear.

Another kind of metaphor which may be at work here would be synaesthesia, which is the process by which different senses are confused: an example would be if I had written above: 'more than the eye can hear or than the ear can see'. An example here, although it is perhaps less acute than a direct substitution of senses, would be in the third stanza: 'Do you take me in, with the milk in the bottom of the bottle'. Here 'take me in' could initially seem to stand for an absorption in terms of the interior senses. It could be asking the question of whether you absorb me into you, contain me in your memories of me, although even there the metaphorical pattern is more complex, since 'take me in' can equally mean 'delude' or 'deceive'. But then this interior movement, whatever it might be, is twisted into a more physical act of absorption, the drinking of milk, which serves further to confuse the reader as to whether it is a mental or physical world which is being described.

The same thing happens earlier in the poem, with the image of the 'swelling light', which may appear at first to be, or at least to allude to, a conventional romantic metaphor whereby the lover sees his beloved as a source of light; but this is rapidly changed ('trans-figured') by the mention of the 'faint bulb', which abruptly returns us to the room, 'de-metaphorises', as it were, the first mention. What is therefore uncanny about these various uses of metaphor is that they conspire to remove the 'ground beneath our feet', to quote the title of one of Rushdie's novels; they place us in a kind of limbo where bodiless voices intersect and echo. Here we see again the proximity of 'metaphor' to 'metamorphosis': metaphor changes the shape of things, although in many cases it does so by reminding us of other shapes of things we have already known; or, as in dream, it gives us the *sense* that we have already known them, even if we have not in any obvious daylight sense done so.

This, then, could bring us back to *déjà-vu*, in the sense that metaphor seeks to 'swell the light', to increase the illumination from the 'faint bulb'; but in doing so it necessarily also places us in a world of shadows, where nothing is exactly as it seems, but also where we seem to know that we have already had intimations that this really is the condition of the world, at least as presented or made present to human perception.

In using the word 'presented', we touch again on a key metaphor of

Fisher's poem, which has to do with presence and absence. If the apparent protagonist is not really 'here', wherever that might be, then it is possible that he might himself be perceived as a 'man-shaped hole in the world', as a shadow-image of himself, as indeed a self which has been drained of self, if by that second self we mean something which is sure of its 'self', sure that there is a way of regarding the world which is metaphor-free.

7

METAPHOR, DIFFERENCE, UNTRANSLATABILITY

Deconstruction is a set of ideas and motifs which can remind us again that the possibility of a full translation, by means of which similarity can be verified, is always under suspension; to say that something is like something else is no longer to *establish* a similarity but to *project* such a similarity into an undecidable field, where the acceptance or recognition of such traces is always at the mercy of a more, or increasingly less, communal readership. The recognition of metaphor thus becomes not only a sign of power but also a powerful marker of cultural instability; metaphors need to be considered not only in terms of their endurance but also in terms of their passing away, their failure to fix language in untenable postures, the ways they have of vacating meanings and leaving us adrift, surrounded only by cliché, metaphor's ideological residue. One relevant question would be: what is a dead metaphor, and how may it be used to commercial and cultural advantage?

In order to explore this further, I want to turn to what may seem a surprising example, one to which I shall return at intervals in this chapter, some stanzas from a lyric by Bob Dylan:

When you're lost in the rain in Juarez and it's Eastertime too
And your gravity fails and negativity don't pull you through
Don't put on any airs when you're down on Rue Morgue Avenue
They got some hungry women there and they really make a mess outa
    you

Now if you see Saint Annie please tell her thanks a lot
I cannot move, my fingers are all in a knot
I don't have the strength to get up and take another shot
And my best friend, my doctor, won't even say what it is I've got

Sweet Melinda, the peasants call her the goddess of gloom
She speaks good English and she invites you up into her room
And you're so kind and careful not to go to her too soon
And she takes your voice and leaves you howling at the moon

Up on Housing Project Hill it's either fortune or fame
You must pick one or the other though neither of them are to be what
    they claim
If you're lookin' to get silly you better go back to from where you came
Because the cops don't need you and man they expect the same

. . .

I started out on burgundy but soon hit the harder stuff
Everybody said they'd stand behind me when the game got rough
But the joke was on me, there was nobody even there to call my bluff
I'm going back to New York City, I do believe I've had enough

(Dylan 1994: 315–16)

In thinking through the metaphorical structure of this lyric, one obvious
starting-place would be Juarez on the Mexican border, antagonistically
coupled with New York City in the final stanza. This is in some sense a
visit, familiar from American literature, to Mexico, and in that sense, again
familiar, a visit to a place which is 'below': in a conventional topography
according to which, metaphorically, the north is superior to the south in
the same way as the head is superior to the body, but also racially, socially,
culturally. This is, as Freud or Hillman would say, a visit to the underworld; and the metaphorical structure of the lyric bears this out. There
is no space here to dwell on all the relevant features; but we can at least

consider Rue Morgue Avenue. What might suitably come to mind is Poe's 'The Murders in the Rue Morgue' (1841), a tale of crime and the beast. This is not to say that Dylan had Poe's text in mind when he wrote the lyric; that is something we shall never know. But it is to point to the ways in which common stocks of metaphor become elaborated.

I use this example in order to introduce the question of how far 'metaphorical correspondence' can go. If we think of the potential metaphorical field of a word like 'lion', for example, then obviously it stretches in many directions. To cast the metaphors in the alternative form of similes, one might think of 'as brave as a lion', 'as strong as a lion'; a zookeeper, perhaps with a rather more intimate relationship with lions, might prefer 'as smelly as a lion'; and with a little stretch of the imagination a visitor from the Planet Zog might opt, albeit perhaps only briefly, for 'as furry as a lion'.

In fact, at the risk of losing sight of Dylan's lyric for a moment, it is worth remaining in the company of our visitor from Zog, because what such a perspective underlines is the way in which, and the extent to which, metaphors function, and can only function, in relation to what Stanley Fish refers to as an 'interpretive community'. In other words, to put it very simply, metaphors are not universals. They depend upon cultural and social perceptions, but we can also go one stage further than this and say that metaphors actually *ground* our perceptions. The lion in English mythology, or the eagle in the corresponding US version, are national symbols; they will always have around them, to readers reading within those traditions, a penumbra which will not be available to readers reading from different cultural positions.

In a very interesting autobiographical novel called *Passage to Juneau* (2000), the travel writer Jonathan Raban, in the course of a lone yacht journey up the northwest coast of North America from Seattle to Alaska, calls attention to the characteristic forms of art practised by the seagoing aboriginals who used to populate the area. He points out that their art can seem strange to later Western eyes, since it sometimes appears to be composed of bits and pieces; in a particular piece of work, for example a woven blanket, we might find as we look closely the representation of an eye here, an ear there, with no apparent connection between them. The reason for this, Raban plausibly suggests, is that since water was so crucial to a people who spent most of their lives on or very near to it, their perception of the world was refracted through water; therefore, their representations of the world around, and consequently their metaphors for that world, reflect the broken, choppy surface of things when seen reflected in the waves.

These people's natural metaphors for life, therefore, consist in images of life on the water. The cycle of life is processed and represented as a sea journey, to the final point of air burial, with the body of the deceased hung high in trees in a canoe. From this kind of example, one might derive the thought that life is itself intrinsically metaphorical; that we make sense of our lives through metaphors which seem appropriate to it. Behind these large cultural metaphors lie vast swaths of cultural assumption: the intensely English metaphor of 'hearts of oak', to take a further but equally maritime example, would not be a thinkable way of construing the world (after all, one might think it meant merely 'hard-hearted' rather than 'brave') unless one knew that oak was the favoured, strongest wood for shipbuilding, and thus available as a cultural metaphor for a concept of power and courage appropriate to a nation which perceived itself, during the eighteenth and nineteenth centuries, when the metaphor came to its fullest fruition, as essentially maritime, dependent on naval supremacy.

To return to Dylan and to problems of translatability: in construing the metaphors in the lyric, it is important, but it is also natural to our reading or listening, to draw limits around the metaphors on offer. For example, the notion of 'Eastertime' clearly sets up a religious thread that crops up more than once in the lyric, for example in the image of 'Saint Annie' in the second stanza. But at the same time, it would be an error of reading to suppose that this is a controlling metaphor that runs through the whole of the lyric. It may indeed inflect the reference to 'Housing Project Hill' in the fourth stanza in such a way as to remind us of the Hill of Calvary, where Jesus was crucified, and it may further underpin a note of suffering that runs through the lyric; but metaphors have limits, and one of the crucial ways in which literature works is by setting one metaphor, or one field of metaphor, against another.

So here, for example, the metaphorisation of Mexico and the metaphorisation of religion enter into a complex interplay. We do not suppose for a moment that sweet Melinda is actually a goddess; neither, probably, because of the undertones of prostitution as a symbol of exploitation in the third stanza, do we seriously suppose that she has many of the attributes of a goddess. Instead, the metaphor functions within a certain field of reference, here to an extent ironic: it is possible to imagine that the lyric's protagonist, searching for a metaphor in which to describe this encounter, comes up with the notion of the goddess, but only in ironised form; the metaphor is used, in fact, not to point to a *similarity* but to a *difference*.

And here is another point at which the whole notion of metaphor becomes complicated, and where the methods of deconstruction can be helpful, because, again put very simply, deconstruction claims that words do not have fixed meanings. Building on the insights of structuralism, deconstruction claims that words, and thus by implication metaphors, are radically unstable; their meanings are always fluid, changing according to historical and cultural context, with the meanings trapped inside them constantly overflowing, refusing to be pinned down. To take the phrase 'howling at the moon', which Dylan is here borrowing from a stock of Negro blues lyrics and which may relate also to the blues singer Howlin' Wolf: the metaphor of the wolf is obvious, but we shall not appreciate the complex force of the metaphor unless we see that alongside its strength of representation there is also a certain 'hollowing out', a way in which, because the metaphor has been used so often, it has lost a great deal of its apparent force. Therefore, a protagonist who claims to be 'howling at the moon' is no longer using the metaphor to indicate a genuine throe of passion, but rather to demonstrate an ironically self-pitying view of a personal plight. This metaphor simultaneously *deepens* and betrays a certain *shallowness*.

'Howling at the moon' might, however, remind us of a further dimension to the relations between, shall we say, metaphor and the human, for it is the case that many of the root metaphors which we come across appear to attempt to establish some parity or opposition between the human and the rest of the animal world. We can stay with the case of the wolf, and with a remark made by Dean Inge (1919: 42–3): 'It takes in reality only one to make a quarrel. It is useless for the sheep to pass resolutions in favour of vegetarianism, while the wolf remains of a different opinion.' Here, a constellation of metaphors involving the wolf is conjured, but principally the 'big bad wolf' of folk legend, which here stands in for all those irresistibly violent and unstable forces that will, perhaps inevitably, upset all plans for human betterment, make sure that our plans 'gang aft agley' (Burns 2001: 96). And this metaphor of wolf also goes back to the roots of Western civilisation, or at least to Romulus and Remus, mythical founders of Rome, who were suckled by a she-wolf. Presumably this signifies that at the origin of civilisation there is a tamed, or at least maternal and nurturing, version of nature which has to be in some sense implicated in the founding act of the civilised. The deployment of this metaphor shows a deep, if unconscious, understanding of the precarious nature of civilisation; it also inevitably demonstrates something quite different, about the relationship between the so-called civilising impulse and the principle of femininity, such that the violence of the male wolf can in some sense be coerced or co-opted by the city as a means of reminding wild nature of its nurturing responsibilities.

And this can readily move us back directly into the heartland of psychoanalytical metaphor, by means of Freud's text *Civilisation and its Discontents* (1930), where he deploys one of the cultural master-metaphors of recent centuries. He details some of the history of Rome down the centuries, and then says:

> Now let us, by a flight of imagination, suppose that Rome is not a human habitation but a psychical entity with a similarly long and copious past – an entity, that is to say, in which nothing that has once come into existence will have passed away and all the earlier phases of development continue to exist alongside the latest ones.
>
> (Freud 1964: 70)

He then goes on to detail what this Rome would be like, with buildings from all centuries and periods (like, we might fairly suppose, the different reference points of Dylan's lyric) superimposed one upon another: 'And the observer would perhaps only have to change the direction of his glance or his position in order to call up the one view or the other' (Freud 1964: 70). Freud means this as an image of the unconscious, from which, according to psychoanalysis, nothing ever goes away. But seen in another light, or deconstructed in another way, we could see it as a metaphor for metaphor itself, in the sense that metaphor constantly reminds us of the *depth* of words, of the ways in which they cannot be separated from their centuries, even millennia, of accreted connotations.

In order to exemplify this depth, I want to introduce some further relevant instances of texts that try to revitalise or rewrite a tradition; a particularly apt example is Jean Rhys's *Wide Sargasso Sea* (1966), and it is interesting to demonstrate the shift in metaphorical structure that marks its 'difference' from Charlotte Brontë's *Jane Eyre* (1847), the text on which it is modelled and whose alternative story it tells. In these two texts, one might suggest, for example, that blindness is a controlling metaphor, but it is deployed quite differently in each. In *Jane Eyre* Rochester goes literally blind as a result of the fire which is the climactic moment of the text. But this blindness also serves a complex metaphorical function. Through a curious reversal, it underlines two further features: first, the equalisation of status which finally allows Rochester and Jane to come together by depriving Rochester of one of the props and guarantees of his superiority. Very near the end, we may recall, Jane says: 'being so much lower of stature than he, I served both for his prop and guide' (Brontë 1966: 473). We are thus reminded by the text that being of 'lower stature', which here metaphorically implies lower social rank as well as being of smaller build, may not only be conceived as a mark of inferiority, but also, or instead, as providing a necessary 'grounding'. The second implication of blindness in *Jane Eyre* is to remind us that Rochester has been blind all along to Jane's virtues. While possessed of sight, he has been unable to avoid being influenced in his relation to her both by her lower social status and by what she herself at least refers to on many occasions as her 'plainness'. It is worth noting that the word 'plain' is, in these contexts, also metaphorical, in that it refers to an admirable plainness of speech as well as a lack, according to conventional ideas, of beauty. Now deprived of sight, these problems fall away, and although it would be going too far to suggest that this new blindness is in some sense a recompense for an older, culturally conditioned blindness, the intensity and structural completeness of the text still owe a great deal to the relations between the two blindnesses.

No text, it is probably safe to say, has a single controlling metaphor; nevertheless, it is striking how these metaphors recur in refigured shape in *Wide Sargasso Sea*, which is essentially a retelling of part of the story of *Jane Eyre* from a narrative perspective close to Rochester's first wife, the 'madwoman in the attic' of *Jane Eyre*. The male protagonist, who is not actually named in the text, newly arrived in the Caribbean, finds sight deeply problematic from the outset: 'Everything is too much, I felt as I rode wearily after her. Too much blue, too much purple, too much green. The flowers too red, the mountains too high, the hills too near' (Rhys

1997: 42). What might otherwise be seen as a set of metaphors for scenic beauty (red flowers, high mountains, green hills) here acquires a quite different set of connotations, as that which afflicts sight, that before which the eye flinches. And this inability to see continues through his dealings with his wife:

> The cold light was on her and I looked at the sad droop of her lips, the frown between her thick eyebrows, deep as if it had been cut with a knife. As I looked she moved and flung her arm out. I thought coldly, yes, very beautiful, the thin wrist, the sweet swell of the forearm, the rounded elbow, the curve of her shoulder into her upper arm. All present, all correct. As I watched, hating, her face grew smooth and very young again, she even seemed to smile. A trick of the light perhaps. What else?
> (Rhys 1997: 88)

Here, there is what one might refer to as a willed blindness, a refusal to see because to see would involve emotional involvement and attachment. The fact that such attachment would be perilous beyond belief is indicated in the second word, in the metaphor of 'cold'; as we look at that word, we can see the various levels of metaphor at stake. Light cannot be cold, any more than it can be hot, according to the laws of physics; if it is cold here, it is because of the way the watcher chooses to construe it, and it is at the same time a description of his own emotional state; or perhaps better of the emotional state into which he is willing himself as he detaches himself from the beauty of her body and resorts to a 'cold' removal from emotion. And so the 'trick of the light': the metaphors here conspire towards a rejection, a refusal to see what is in front of him. We might consider also 'deep as if it had been cut with a knife'. This represents not only, or indeed perhaps not at all, a physical feature; instead, the metaphor of cutting moves us towards an understanding of the protagonist's half-suppressed wish to wound the girl, to damage her beauty, while at the same time, because of the precise positioning of the wound, suggesting a damage to sight, perhaps to his sight of her, which wounds his self-esteem; or perhaps to her own sight, because to be looked at by her makes him feel belittled.

'None so blind as will not see': so goes the old cliché; and it has to be repeated (as I have tried to evidence in the Dylan lyric) that the study of metaphor necessarily involves engaging with clichés, because clichés are frequently themselves metaphors which have been overused. But blindness itself, as well as the act or process of blinding, has almost endless extensions through Western textuality. It is eventually founded on the all-encompassing metaphor of 'enlightenment', insofar as it stands in for understanding, a term which is itself a metaphor. In shorthand terms, enlightenment in Western cultural mythology stands for resisting the darkness which is itself a metaphor for incomprehension, or a failure to grasp. Whereas *Jane Eyre* offers daylight to Jane as a result of Rochester's blinding, the protagonist of *Wide Sargasso Sea*, the alternative Rochester, has in the end to flee the site of too much sight, a sight which if he were to apprehend it correctly would fatally compromise the stability of his world. And hence the metaphor offered in the title of the novel, the 'Sargasso Sea', which mythologically stands in for a place where things are lost, where there is nothing on which to ground one's perceptions.

A further example of this rewriting of tradition, of remaking a text in the context of what Derrida calls *différance*, may be found in Blake's famous rewriting of John Milton in *The Marriage of Heaven and Hell* (1793). Blake was involved over more or less the whole of his writing life, and indeed also as an engraver and painter, with Milton, a writer whom he simultaneously loved and feared. In Plates 5–6 of *The Marriage of Heaven and Hell* Blake says that the history of the relations between reason and desire is written in Milton's *Paradise Lost* (1667–74):

> But in Milton, the Father is Destiny, the Son a Ratio of the five senses, & the Holy-ghost Vacuum!
> Note: The reason Milton wrote in fetters when he wrote of Angels & God, and at liberty when of Devils & Hell, is because he was a true Poet and of the Devil's party without knowing it.
>
> (Blake 1966: 150)

In this brief comment, Blake seeks to undo the whole of Milton's metaphorical structure, thereby endeavouring to demonstrate that metaphors themselves are time-bound and ideologically motivated. But, says Blake, even though Milton tried his hardest to demonstrate the goodness of God and the evil of the Devil, he was undone by his own writing, by the way in which his own metaphors were far more vivid when treating of Satan and his rebel angels than when treating of God and Jesus.

One of the crucial phrases here is 'without knowing it'. We might say that Blake is formulating a very early version of structuralism, in the sense that he is saying we cannot bend language to our will; language itself will always be stronger and will speak *through* our words rather than being bound by them. The metaphor of 'fetters' is clearly crucial in this respect.

Blake's aim here, as in many other parts of his work, is to recast, reforge, metaphor. Obviously, it would not be appropriate here to go into detail as to how he does that, or to quote the many other examples of his rewritings of biblical and Miltonic texts; but it is worth pointing out that he mounts a direct challenge to any notion of the stable authority of meaning, and in doing so prefigures deconstructionist arguments about fixity and fluidity, about the inevitable 'dissemination' of words, and in this case, because of the theological argument which underpins this passage, of 'the Word'.

It is significant that one of those arguments would be the one advanced by Derrida in his essay 'Edmond Jabès and the Question of the Book' (1964), where he says:

> *Absence* of the writer too. For to write is to draw back. Not to retire into one's tent, in order to write, but to draw back from one's writing itself. To be grounded far from one's language, to emancipate it or lose one's hold on it, to let it make its way alone and unarmed. To leave speech. To be a poet is to know how to leave speech. To let it speak alone, which it can do only in its written form. *To leave* writing is to be there only in order to provide its passageway, to be the diaphanous element of its going forth: everything and nothing. For the work, the writer is at once everything and nothing. Like God.
>
> (Derrida 1978b: 70)

This takes up in one sense Blake's highly idiosyncratic theology, and perhaps especially his constant insistence that his work was the responsibility of spirits who spoke through him as much as it was of his own craftsmanlike efforts to give their words mortal form. But it also goes further than this, in implicitly suggesting that the very process of metaphoricity has been wrongly conceived. For Derrida, it would follow that metaphor is not that which happens when the writer applies him- or herself to the craft; it is what happens when there is a drawing back, a willingness, conscious or unconscious, to let go of the writing, to abandon it to its fate. Metaphor, therefore, is not necessarily embedded in the text; it is rather a mark of what happens to the text when it achieves its freedom, which will only be in the company of other readers, other places, other times.

This is a difficult thought to grasp: much critical training lies in the idea that if we can descry and gather together the key metaphorical components of a work, then we can use this as a beginning of our interpretation. But what both Blake and Derrida suggest is rather that as we read and 'absorb' literature, the metaphorical structure of the work we are reading becomes, to use Blake's key-word, 'forged' anew.

The ambiguity of Blake's notion of forging should not be lost on us. On the one hand, it signifies forging in the sense of the blacksmith's forge, the sense of iron-making and, by metaphorical translation, imposing some formed solidity on the flux of life. But, on the other hand, it implies virtually its exact opposite, namely the act of forgery; not perhaps in the sense of conscious deception but rather as an acknowledgement that all our attempts at originality are in fact suspect, held, as Derrida would say, *sous rature*, 'under erasure' (Derrida 1976: 19), because they can figure only as part of a continuing palimpsest, beneath the later stages of which there are always other texts, other perceptions, other translations, shadows hovering on the edges of visibility.

We might consider a comment by the Nobel Prize-winning novelist Saul Bellow: 'A novel is balanced between a few true impressions and the multitude of false ones that make up most of what we call life. It tells us that for every human being there is a diversity of existences, that the single existence is itself an illusion' (Bellow in Allen 1993: 142). This points us towards the inevitability of forgery as part of the essence of fiction; and we can place alongside the critic David Lodge's famous comment on the American novelist Herman Melville, author of *Moby-Dick* (1851). Melville, he said, 'split the atom of the traditional novel in the effort to make whaling a universal metaphor' (Lodge 1975: 195). We might take from Lodge's comment that, in fact, no attempt to construct a truly universal metaphor can wholly succeed, for obvious reasons of cultural diversity and difference; but that, nevertheless, the effort to construct such metaphors, or to revitalise them, or to reforge them for particular times and places, is also integral to literature, even if here it is, in some sense, safeguarded by being itself couched in the Promethean metaphor of heroic struggle.

8

METAPHOR AND THE POSTCOLONIAL TURN

The question of what to compare with what is therefore in no sense a universal or natural one, but one that is guided by strict lines of power. This has been made increasingly clear by postcolonial writers as they describe their ambiguous difficulties with language, especially with the English language which, composed as it is of specific power- and history-laden metaphors, provides a field of connections to be resisted and reconsidered at the same time as it is mined and exploited for its still potent metaphorical field. To call a yam a sweet potato is fundamentally different from calling a potato a sour yam. Metaphor here becomes inextricably involved with the history of what it means to be regarded as exotic, a process according to which the other comes to be conceived as the filling in of a missing ideal, the establishment of a new space to compensate for a metaphorical lack; metaphor reveals its relation to a web of notions of loss.

But perhaps it is best to start from a text which long precedes the development of postcolonial awareness, Henry Newbolt's most celebrated work, 'Vitaï Lampada' (meaning 'Torch of Life'), written in 1897 about a schoolboy who grows up to fight in African wars:

> There's a breathless hush in the Close to-night –
> Ten to make and the match to win –
> A bumping pitch and a blinding light,
> An hour to play and the last man in.
> And it's not for the sake of a ribboned coat,
> Or the selfish hope of a season's fame,
> But his Captain's hand on his shoulder smote –
> 'Play up! play up! and play the game!'
>
> The sand of the desert is sodden red, –
> Red with the wreck of a square that broke; –
> The Gatling's jammed and the Colonel dead,
> And the regiment blind with dust and smoke.
> The river of death has brimmed his banks,
> And England's far, and Honour a name,
> But the voice of a schoolboy rallies the ranks:
> 'Play up! play up! and play the game!'
>
> This the word that year by year,
> While in her place the School is set,
> Every one of her sons must hear,
> And none that hears it dare forget.
> This they all with a joyful mind
> Bear through life like a torch in flame,
> And falling fling to the host behind –
> 'Play up! play up! and play the game!'
>
> (Newbolt 1907: 86–7)

Clearly this poem is a metaphorical structure; the game of cricket is set in a metaphorical relation to war, the assertion being that the way to play cricket is also the way to fight. Interestingly, one of the effects of this metaphorical constellation is to complicate the reader's sense of time. We might ask: are we positioned with the grown-up ex-schoolboy on the field of battle, or are we positioned back in the school with the battle merely an example of the kind of situation in which the school's teachings will, perhaps, have their due effect? In some cases, this metaphorical elision is drawn even closer together; for example, the 'Captain' of the first stanza appears literally to be the captain of the cricket team, but could just as easily be read as a military officer.

But in a sense every phrase here can be *read double* through the metaphorical process. 'A bumping pitch and a blinding light', a phrase partially echoed by 'the regiment blind with dust and smoke' in the second stanza, can also serve to describe, through a kind of uncanny premonition, the conditions of desert warfare which are singularly inhospitable to the British soldier. Similarly, the 'ribboned coat', while it might signify the regalia to be worn by a member of the school team, can equally serve as a description redolent of medals of gallantry such as might be acquired by conspicuously brave behaviour on the field of battle.

The 'red' in the first two lines of the second stanza also serves a double metaphorical function: on the one hand, it refers to blood and thus to the wounds and deaths of the battle; on the other, it refers to the red uniforms of the British soldiery. In the course of drawing the two together, being a member of the British army is made to imply a patriotic willingness to suffer and die for one's country. The 'river of death', we notice, is personalised ('his banks'), a personification which is another type of metaphor and here serves to give an anthropomorphic turn to the processes of death, recalling the human adversaries of the cricket match. Indeed, it is interesting to notice that this personification of death serves also to reinforce the depersonalisation of the enemy, who nowhere appear in the poem: the game is not one which is played, or played out, between living, human adversaries, but rather a more internalised matter of living up to, and dying for, a code of honour, even when that 'Honour' is merely a 'name', in the sense that any honour shown on this battlefield is unlikely to be noticed or commended. Thus, in a move familiar from a host of imperialist texts, the enemy is dehumanised and the real battle shown is not so much against that enemy as a constant war within the self to live up to, or let down, a set of principles which stretch from public-school education through to behaviour on the battlefield.

It is not, of course, literally the 'voice of a schoolboy' that rallies the ranks; rather, it is, presumably, a voice which is imbued with a set of values learnt *as* a schoolboy, and by implication not a cultural voice which might be available to the 'ranks', in the sense of the lesser soldiers under his charge. We notice too the way in which the 'School' of stanza three is capitalised. We might refer to this as a kind of hypostasisation, or making of a concept into an object, which is a further kind of metaphor; this is no mere individual 'school', but rather a bundle of attitudes and principles signified by the concept 'School', a set of notions which is thereby elevated above other possible principles, and this is intensified by the idea that the School has 'sons'. A school does not literally have sons, although it might educate people who are themselves sons, and not, in this case, daughters. But the metaphor emphasises that the relation between the school and its pupils is quasi-familial. There is a literal truth behind this in the sense that the great Victorian schools had a symbiotic relationship with empire, in that it was precisely the sons of those on imperial service who formed the mainstay of the clientele for such schools; it was thus culturally critical to assert that even though these sons are in some sense deprived of familial comfort, nevertheless this is in the service of a greater good. Thus, a whole concept of generation and succession is asserted as these sons acquire the mindset that will make them fit followers in their fathers' footsteps, whether on the field of battle in Africa or in the Anglo-Indian Civil Service.

The 'torch in flame' is a metaphor which seeks to capture a whole history of Western civilisation, through its reference back to the Olympic spirit and also through its connection to the title of the poem, 'Vitaï Lampada', the lamp or light of life, in the sense of a guiding principle which will serve to guide one through life's worst difficulties, even, as in 'falling', to the point of death. The importance of these metaphors in asserting a historical and generational succession is finally emphasised in the penultimate line: the 'hosts behind' are, presumably, the further ranks of soldiers who will come to occupy the places of those killed, but they are also the rising ranks of the young who will come to replenish the diminishing stocks of British soldiery, and here specifically of the officer class, available for imperial warfare.

It is essential to grasp that postcolonial texts, reworking this kind of already inhabited metaphorical terrain, coin new metaphors or, very frequently, adapt and change existing ones. A classic case is the novel *Things Fall Apart* (1958), by the West African writer Chinua Achebe. Here, we are immediately plunged into a metaphorical field with the presence of an opening quotation from W.B. Yeats's poem 'The Second Coming' (1921):

> Turning and turning in the widening gyre
> The falcon cannot hear the falconer;

> Things fall apart; the centre cannot hold;
> Mere anarchy is loosed upon the world.
>   (Yeats 1965: 210–11)

The most obvious metaphors here are to do with the 'gyre', a favourite one of Yeats's, and the falcon and the falconer. Most readings of the poem would agree that these metaphors are intended to suggest a condition of global, or at least of European, politics in which old assumptions are decaying and, consequently, there is a vacuum into which evil may flow. The unhearing falcon represents a loss of control, and specifically, as the metaphor develops, a loss of control from 'the centre'.

But what is meant by 'the centre'? It would appear likely that Yeats means a kind of consensus, that kind of consensus to which, according to certain ways of thinking, all reasonable people could, or should, adhere. But as Achebe's novel develops and we are forced to re-evaluate the concept of 'the centre', the metaphor changes its force. It would be fair to say that in Achebe's work the centre is itself perceived, if not as a malignant force, then at the very least as responsible for the very social, political and cultural problems now being encountered in Africa, and perhaps globally. And this is in part a question of perspective. What is revealed is that Yeats's metaphor makes (its original) sense only if the world is perceived 'under Western eyes' (Conrad 1991), to use a metaphor from a different source. If the centre is itself relocated as an oppressive phenomenon, as representing a view of the world which is itself profoundly Eurocentric, then indeed the events the novel discloses may be perceived as 'anarchy' from this perspective; the task of the postcolonial writer then becomes the disclosure of other points of view, other perspectives from which to develop the metaphor in the way it has been developed by many postcolonial writers and critics, the 'margins' which will shift the metaphor into, as it were, a different gear. Thus, metaphor is itself to be seen as perspectival, or, to put it another way, as ideological; the force of a metaphor will depend on its accepted interpretation from the point of view of the dominant class or culture.

Dreadful events occur in *Things Fall Apart*, and the novel is in part an attempt to allow the reader to see these events from an African rather than from a Western perspective. But while these events are unfolding, the white District Commissioner is writing a book in which he is retelling these events from his own point of view; the title of his book, which he decides upon at the end of the novel, is *The Pacification of the Primitive Tribes of the Lower Niger*. This, then, is an attempt to retell the events from his own viewpoint and, in the process, to coin a different series of metaphors. The term 'primitive', for example, bears a host of metaphorical allusions, according to which the actually extremely complex social structures of the African tribes are reduced to something historically early, something which must be rejected and surpassed in the name of development. But we can go further than this. 'The Lower Niger' may be a geographical term, although, like most geographical terms, it is actually a Western imposition; but in the context of the novel, the term 'lower' also bears the freight of its metaphorical associations with 'debased', 'primitive', and so forth. Similarly, the term 'Niger' itself, whatever the original meaning ascribed to it by Western explorers and cartographers, will in this new context inevitably cast up associations with the derogatory term 'nigger'; thus, a set of assumptions about 'blackness', and about European fear and incomprehension in the face of blackness, is brought to the surface. When the term 'pacification' is mentioned, its metaphorical connotations extend beyond the assumptions of the inaccurately perceived warlike notion of the black African, for 'pacifier' is also an alternative term for a baby's dummy; thus, a metaphorical association is made between African peoples and infancy.

Metaphor thus becomes, crucially, a contested field; it also becomes visible as a weapon in the ideological armoury by means of which history is interpreted, or reinterpreted, from the perspective of the conqueror. We might consider a passage from the novel:

> Large crowds began to gather on the village *ilo* as soon as the edge had worn off the sun's heat and it was no longer painful on the body. Most communal ceremonies took place at that time of the day, so that even when it was said that a ceremony would begin 'after the midday meal' everyone understood that it would begin a long time later, when the sun's heat had softened.
>
> (Achebe 1958: 63)

Here, the writer is placing himself in the position of an interpreter of metaphors. 'After the midday meal' does not mean exactly what it says, or at least it does not mean what it would generally be assumed to mean by a Western observer; but the force of the metaphor is entirely comprehensible to the culture within which the metaphor has evolved, to the consternation of those trying to impose a different time scheme on the native peoples. Similarly, Achebe refers to a young man growing 'like a yam tendril in the rainy season', and being 'full of the sap of life'. The first metaphor, in this case a simile, is one which is firmly located in the life experience of the tribe, and is not one which would occur to people living in different cultural conditions; the second metaphor, of the sap, *can* be found in Western literature, but here its proximity to the first metaphor enables it to contribute to a different picture.

We might consider another example, and there is a good reason for doing so, because just as Achebe's text is attempting to change a hierarchy of discourse, so too, in an apparently very different context, were the English metaphysical poets. John Donne's poem 'The Apparition' (1633) centres on the idea that the narrator, having been scorned by the woman who is the poem's addressee, will return to haunt her:

> When by thy scorne, O murderess, I am dead,
> And that thou think'st thee free
> From all solicitation from me,
> Then shall my ghost come to thy bed,
> And thee, feigned vestal, in worse armes shall see
> (Donne 1990: 118)

Here, it would seem probable that Donne is using the notion of the ghost as a metaphor for his own, or rather his protagonist's own, thoughts of revenge for the lady's resistance to his advances. Even this makes certain historical assumptions about what we might think of as the literality status of spirits; but a thorough reading of Donne's poetry would still support this view. What is certain about this metaphor, however, is that it is an imposition of some kind; the return of the ghost is meant to be taken in some sense more literally by the victim of the apparition, certainly more frighteningly, than it is by the poet, for whom the concept of the ghost is the hinge for a display of metaphysical wit. Here again, we see the notion of the metaphor as a communicative act; the metaphorical status of the metaphor constitutes an act of sharing between the poet and his readership, but at the expense, very much in the same way as Freud's assumption of the lower status of the non-sharer of the joke, of the person to whom the poem is 'addressed'. I put the word 'addressed' in inverted commas because we need to see that the force-field of the metaphor enhances a question about to whom the poem actually *is* addressed: is the 'major addressee' the woman or the reader? At all events, this metaphor works within its historical range, and indeed that historical range is long: the notion of ghosts as embodiments of vengeance stretches from ancient times, through Donne and Shakespeare, emblematically in *Hamlet* (1601), to present times in such fictions as those by Stephen King.

We might not think of Donne as a poet who has much to do with the concept of the colony, but in fact this was a master-trope for the metaphysical poets. What is more important here, however, is to say that in continuing to think about the 'postcolonial turn', but especially in terms of the ever-absorbing topic of ghosts, we naturally run up against differences in sets of belief structures, and consequent relocations of metaphor. One of the most startling Anglophone writers of the twentieth century was Amos Tutuola. He, like Achebe, was a Nigerian, a blacksmith by trade and a teller of stories, some of which were written down, perhaps with the help of his publisher or of other intermediaries. One of his best-known books is *The Palm-Wine Drinkard, and his dead Palm-Wine Tapster in the Deads' Town* (1952). Here, the question of the metaphorical status of ghosts and spirits becomes extremely complicated. For example, a chapter called 'Not Too Small to be Chosen' begins with the following paragraph:

> There were many wonderful creatures in the olden days. One day, the king of the 'Wraith-Island' town chose all the people, spirits and terrible creatures of the Island to help him to clear his corn field which was about 2 miles square. Then one fine morning, we gathered together and went to the corn field, and cleared it away, after that, we returned to the king and told him that we had cleared his corn field, he thanked us, and gave us food and drinks.
>
> (Tutuola 1952: 48–9)

What is fascinatingly unclear here, we might say, is the status and meaning of 'we'. Does the writer mean us to suppose that this 'we' includes the 'spirits and terrible creatures'? It would appear so; in which case these beings are operating on the same dimension as the 'people'; there is no distinction to be drawn between human agents and beings from what we might, from a different cultural perspective, consider to be a quite different metaphysical realm.

Is this passage in any sense metaphorical, or should we rather say that any metaphoricity that is attributable to it is an effect not of the writing but of the reading, and consequently reception, of the text within a different cultural field? This is a question that can be applied to the whole book, which throughout assumes an interaction of the mortal and the immortal that seems quite foreign to Western presumptions. The attribution of metaphor here again becomes indissolubly linked with assumptions about cultural supremacy; it would, to think back to Achebe's ironised terms, be only a so-called primitive people who could accept such a concept literally. Indeed, we might also say that the very thought of *thinking literally* is usually, in our culture, a gesture of dismissal; we are not supposed to think literally, for to do so betrays an unawareness of the slipping and sliding possibilities of language. We have come a long way from that system of thought which regarded the clarity of the literal as a goal to be desired, and metaphor as a potentially delusive ornament which, although it might aid persuasiveness, was at root a derogation from the attainable goal of a speech so clear and pure that it could hold up a distortion-free mirror to nature.

Let us consider one more passage from Tutuola. This is to do with a curious episode where 'fear' and 'death' are bought from the protagonist, a protagonist who is frequently plural:

> Then we took our 'fear' back from the borrower and he paid us the last interest on it. Then we found the one who had bought our 'death' and told him to bring it, but he told us that he could not return it again, because he bought it from us and had paid for it already, so we left our 'death' for the buyer, so we took only our 'fear'.
>
> (Tutuola 1952: 71)

What is apparent in this passage is that there is a metaphorical field at work. Seen from one perspective, it is evident in the inverted commas which surround the words 'fear' and 'death'. Seen more broadly, one could say that a discourse of fear and death is metaphorically related to a discourse which is essentially drawn from usury, capitalism, and the notion of 'interest' interpreted in a monetary sense. But which of these is the vehicle and which the tenor of the metaphor? Here, I suggest, it is impossible to say. We cannot simply say that Tutuola is using the rhetoric of capitalism and 'interest' to shed light upon, or bring to bear our attention upon, a different psychological or philosophical realm; neither can we say simply that all this is an extended metaphor *for* capitalism and the inroads which it has made upon traditional African values and assumptions. Both of these views might (to use a relevant metaphor) have some *currency*; but neither can explain or interpret the density of metaphoric relation contained in the passage.

A very different example we might consider, but one which also challenges our ability to cope, as readers, with different registers of discourse, is the first stanza of the Caribbean writer Derek Walcott's poem 'Elegy' (1969):

Our hammock swung between Americas,
we miss you, Liberty. Che's
bullet-riddled body falls,
and those who cried, the Republic must first die
to be reborn, are dead,
the freeborn citizen's ballot in the head.
Still, everybody wants to go to bed
With Miss America. And, if there's no bread,
let them eat cherry pie.

(Walcott 1992: 109)

This passage is perhaps best described as an amalgam of metaphors, or even as an *amalgamated metaphor*. Among its constituent parts are images drawn from seafaring (the hammock) and its connotations of the slave trade; images from the South American liberations of the 1960s and 1970s (the mention of 'Che' can hardly fail to call to mind both the life and actions of Che Guevara and also his encapsulation in Western posters and other imagery); the Statue of Liberty and all the promise and betrayal it has signified over the years; and with 'Miss America' and 'cherry pie', a set of images of wholesome US nationalism and patriotism.

All of these metaphors, or metaphorical elements, are here conjoined, jammed together, so that it becomes, in this new postcolonial coinage, difficult if not impossible to know what is a metaphor for what. What is certain is that none of these metaphors will be individually satisfactory, none will serve to capture the in-between state that Walcott is attempting to portray: as well as being between countries and between nationalities, Walcott is attempting to capture in the Caribbean context the sense of being *between metaphors*, of finding none of them adequate. They may have a splendid sound, but behind or within them there is a certain hollowness, a failure to live up to the public ideal which the metaphor proclaims. As we observe the metaphor, it swings around like a coin revealing its obverse side; we see that the metaphor is itself a cover story for the processes of history, and it becomes the task of the poet, if not necessarily to deconstruct these metaphors, at least to relocate them in a place where their claims can be more fully and properly examined.

A little later in the poem come these lines:

> and yearly lilacs in her dooryards bloom,
> and the cherry orchard's surf
> blinds Washington and whispers
> to his assassin in his furnished room
> of an ideal America, whose flickering screens
> show, in slow herds, the ghosts of the Cheyennes
> scuffling across the staked and wired plains
> with whispering, rag-bound feet,
>
> while the farm couple framed in their Gothic door
> like Calvin's saints, waspish, pragmatic, poor,
> gripping the devil's pitchfork
> stare rigidly towards the immortal wheat.
>
> (Walcott 1992: 109–10)

Here, Walcott sets up a kind of compendium of images of America, but the most important thing about them, from the dooryard lilacs, through Washington, through the ghosts of the Indians on the 'staked and wired plains' and on to the farm couple from classic American painting, is that they are, as it were, America's own metaphors for itself, emphasising and foregrounding those sorts of quality and virtue which are reckoned to make up the white American character. The fact, however, that these metaphors are not stable is pointed up by the use of 'whispers'/'whispering'; the apparently solid, even 'rigid' metaphor is in fact haunted by its own other, by a voice seeking different metaphors, a voice that cannot be fully silenced but remains to haunt the metaphoric structure.

9

SOME EXAMPLES AND LIMITS

The postcolonial, then, represents a kind of limiting case for the use of metaphor and its connections with discourse and power. In this chapter, I want to turn to some different examples of limits, and to begin by considering a single verse paragraph from a poem, 'The Oval Window' (1983), by one of the most difficult writers in modern English, J.H. Prynne:

> Her wrists shine white like the frosted snow;
> they call each other to the south stream.
> The oval window is closed in life,
> by the foot-piece of the stapes. Chill shadows
> fall from the topmost eaves, clear waters
> run inside the blossoming peach. Inside
> this window is the perilymph of the vestibule.
>   Now O now I needs must part,
>   parting though I absent mourne.
> It is a child's toy, shaken back in
> myopic eddies by the slanting bridge:
> toxic; dangerous fire risk; bright moonlight
> floods the steps like a cascade of water.
>
> (Prynne 2005: 331)

One thing that is immediately apparent here is that the reader is not being invited to deal with and interpret individual metaphors, but rather to recognise a whole set of metaphorical levels which could, looked at from a different angle, be thought of as registers of discourse. This is signalled in, for example, the mention of 'stapes' and 'perilymph', which are references to the physiology of the inner ear. It would be possible to point to at least one, maybe two, more metaphorical levels: there are the references, possibly stylised, to Chinese or Japanese writing in, for example, the mention of the 'blossoming peach'; and, perhaps differentiated from this, there is a level of what we might call the 'wintry', which conjures up different scenes, a different background altogether.

This is not the place to attempt an interpretation of these lines of poetry; my point, rather, is to suggest that they challenge, as does the whole of Prynne's work and that of other British and US postmodernist poets from Charles Olson onwards, any notion of metaphor which continues to try to think in terms of vehicle and tenor. If that model has ever been valid (and, as we have seen above, it has been subject to repeated questioning), it would seem that here it falls altogether. The first line, for example, seems at first glance to offer a very beautiful but structurally clear simile, of a kind that we might expect to find in quite conventional love poetry. But whereas under such conventions we might expect this description of female elegance to be pursued in the ensuing lines, the apparent tenor of the metaphor disappears altogether. The vehicle perhaps recurs, but only in muted form; instead the lines go on to roam through other fields of discourse, and the question of metaphor becomes increasingly difficult to discern.

To take the references to the inner ear: we might want to suggest that the physiological discourse used here is metaphorical, but when we ask ourselves why we think this, the answer probably boils down to the thought that nobody ever writes poems about the inner ear, or at least not as physiologically conceived. This is clearly inadequate, and as we ponder its inadequacy we can perhaps sense a whole apparatus of interpretation, and consequently of metaphor, crumbling, because it is not clear that this poem is 'about' anything at all. It is rather a complex text or weaving of language, or languages. It would be possible to excise a sentence like 'Inside/this window is the perilymph of the vestibule', and wonder what difference this excision would make.

This is not for a moment to say that there is anything weak, incoherent or ill-formed here. It is rather to point to the notion of poetry as an 'open field', in which the presumed hierarchical arrangement of discourses is confounded. The very notion of metaphor has, as we have seen, constantly implied that one thing can stand for something else; but even to say that makes a further, realist assumption, that there is a further 'something else' to stand for. Prynne's poetry is a radical rejection of this assumed realism; it is a tissue, a text, a weaving of literary and linguistic allusions. 'Her wrists shine white like the frosted snow', certainly, stands out as a simile; but if we were to assume that the point of the simile is to say something about 'her', or even about the 'frosted snow', we would find ourselves in a state of confusion. Or, to take another sequence of images: the 'oval window' which is 'closed in life' is, we might surmise, the ear itself, our evidence being the mention of the 'stapes'; but in the following sentence it seems as though this oval window has migrated to a different location, no longer physiological but to do with a house in a winter landscape. The 'clear waters' could in some sense be the fluids of the inner ear, and the 'blossoming peach' could be the ear's outward appearance; but to refer such images backwards in this way would surely be to run counter to the poem's own development of this landscape and the pictorial traditions within which it sits.

The last line, we see, contains the word 'steps', and no doubt our eye flicks back to the 'stapes'; indeed, 'stapes' could in fact be a recognisable early medieval plural of the word we now know as 'step', although the etymological history is confusing. Again, the notion of the steps being flooded might remind us of a disorder of the inner ear, but to claim that one of these discourses contains metaphors to be interpreted in terms of the other would violate the codes by which this poetry operates. Perhaps the most difficult statement is one of the simplest: 'It is a child's toy'. *What* is a child's toy? If this is a metaphor, it has little in the way of an identifiable antecedent, but perhaps this is the point. Where metaphor depends upon its own root metaphor of translation, whereby the more strange and the less strange are brought into some kind of harmony, here we seem to have moved beyond metaphor. If we ask the question again, '*What* is a child's toy?', the answer that comes back is: 'A child's toy.' We, as readers, may need more than this: we may, for example, want to say, well, perhaps what is happening here is that life as a whole is being compared to a child's toy, 'shaken back in/myopic eddies', and thus at the mercy of greater forces. But this, I would argue, is again a *recuperative* reading; in other words, it is one which seeks to avoid the dangerous openness of the poetry and to convert it back into an overtly humanistic discourse. By this I mean to point again to the notion that writing is a constant *struggle*: it is certainly amenable to human shaping, but the words themselves operate in a realm which is largely outside our control – the best we can do is to engage with language on its own terms and, some poets would say, to be modest in the light of its power.

Perhaps this move back towards a humanistic discourse is inevitable; certainly, looked at psychoanalytically, one might say that it is a move designed to avoid the terror of the dark, the uncertainties which would attend us if our supposed, even our hallucinated, grip on language were to fail. Our sense of mastery is conferred by our ability to handle language, to use it in order to provide interpretations of the world and of our experience; there is not much space for W.S. Graham's intimations that it is, in fact, the language which is using *us*. But metaphor, if it is indeed a usable tool in our handling of the world, is at best a highly ambiguous one. Instead of sorting the world out into neat order, it is continually proposing correspondences, overlaps, sometimes alarming incongruities, and it cannot be bound by mere issues of history or geography.

How might these problems be limited by the writer? For the writer is, perhaps, always engaged in limiting the endless powers of language rather than in using or 'exploiting' it. We might consider, for example, the opening section of Geoffrey Hill's thirty-section poem, *Mercian Hymns* (1971):

> King of the perennial holly-groves, the riven sand-
> stone: overlord of the M5: architect of the his-
> toric rampart and ditch, the citadel at Tamworth,
> the summer hermitage in Holy Cross: guardian of
> the Welsh Bridge and the Iron Bridge: contractor
> to the desirable new estates: saltmaster: money-
> changer: commissioner for oaths: martyrologist:
> the friend of Charlemagne.

> 'I liked that', said Offa, 'sing it again'.

> (Hill 1971: n.p.)

The scenario of the poem sequence, it will already be obvious, is the West Midlands, the location of the historical kingdom of Mercia, of which Offa was probably the most famous monarch. But what we see here is a more or less total collapse of conventional boundaries of time, so that the at least partly mythic ancient Britain conjured up by the 'perennial holly-groves' sits side by side with the M5, and the 'citadel' at Tamworth rubs shoulders with the modern buildings of the 'desirable new estates'. At least equally important is that this is not just an uncanny juxtaposition of times but also a fracturing and rearranging of discourses and registers: the 'desirable new estates', for example, may or may not be desirable in themselves, depending on who is seeing or living in them; but the *language* of 'desirable new estates' is certainly the language of the modern estate agent and sits with deliberate unease alongside the 'perennial holly-groves', with their mystical and antiquarian associations.

Offa's realm, therefore, is metaphorically extended: it is as though, rather as also with Freud's city of Rome, we (the readers) are seeing a wide array of different chronologies condensed into a single perspective. But at the same time this vision re-echoes backwards and acts upon Offa himself through his own name, as in the second section:

A pet-name, a common name. Best-selling brand, curt
    graffito. A laugh; a cough. A syndicate. A specious
    gift. Scoffed-at horned phonograph.

The starting-cry of a race. A name to conjure with.

There is no space here to go into all the various metaphorical meanings Hill is ascribing to the name, or the word, 'Offa', but one example might suffice to show the density of the poetry, the 'starting-cry of a race', which clearly signifies the sound of the 'off' as a running race begins but also signifies the 'origin' of a race, of the Mercians, and perhaps, by metaphorical extension, of the human race itself insofar as Offa, his kingdom and his deeds are, to use a conventional phrase, lost in the mists of time, uncertain in their own origin. Here, the language is being speculatively remade, or we might perhaps better say that the intrinsic necessity of language to spread out beyond its apparently proper scope of signification, the scope to which centuries of literary theorists and thinkers have done their best to confine it, is being accepted and exploited even though, we might suspect, Hill is also hinting that this 'gift' of language might well be 'specious'.

What we see at work in this willingness to explore the metaphorical duplicities of language might also be described as a certain playfulness. If we were to return for a moment to the Greek theorists, then we would find that their major concern was with decorum and good sense, with arranging words in order and making sure that they neither exceeded their station nor drew undue attention to themselves: words, indeed, on this model were in exactly the same situation as the citizens of a model society, knowing their place and remaining in good order. One might even say, therefore, that a theory of metaphor, or one which, for example, seeks to separate metaphor out as a permissible but fundamentally frivolous adjunct to correct speech, is itself offering a theory of metaphor as a metaphor for society as a whole, as conceived by the writer. If this is the case, then the view that Hill offers is clearly very different. Writing in the wake of the many fragmentations of modernism, he appears more concerned to let metaphors have or appear to have a life of their own. Consider, for example, the seventh section:

> Gasholders, russet among fields. Milldams, marlpools
>   that lay unstirring. Eel-swarms. Coagulations of
>   frogs: once, with branches and half-bricks, he
>   battered a ditchful; then sidled away from the
>   stillness and silence.

> Ceolred was his friend and remained so, even after
>   the day of the lost fighter: a biplane, already
>   obsolete and irreplaceable, two inches of heavy
>   snub silver. Ceolred let it spin through a hole
>   in the classroom-floorboards, softly, into the
>   rat-droppings and coins.

> After school he lured Ceolred, who was sniggering
>   with fright, down to the old quarries, and flayed
>   him. Then, leaving Ceolred, he journeyed for hours,
>   calm and alone, in his private derelict sandlorry
>   named *Albion*.

The scene here is perhaps of the young Offa; but it is also obviously an account of happenings in the life of a modern child. But one is not a metaphor for the other. It is rather as though they merge, or half-merge, partly through the child's own imagination. It appears improbable that Offa, at least in his modern incarnation, *actually* 'flayed' Ceolred; and if indeed he did, it would seem at least as improbable that he then went off to play calmly on his own. But all this is hardly the point. What Hill is conjuring up in this section is a composite and complex metaphor for the child's imagination, where events like flaying, which might appear enormous to the adult world, appear trivial; and where events that are trivial to adults – the loss, for example, of a toy plane – attain horrendous proportions.

The imagination, we might then say, here becomes a metaphor for history: just as the imagination seeks ways of connecting the phenomena with which it is confronted, so history itself is, seen from one angle, a jumble or tangle of disconnected events which the historian or the poet tries to arrange in some semblance of order. The 'coins' here are emblematic: on the one hand, they signify all that which has been irrecoverably lost with the passage of time; on the other, they signify precisely the opposite, for they are among the few artefacts which are, in fact, continually being found and which go a long way to make up the repository of antique objects from which at least some small parts of distant history might be reconstructed. That the presumably toy lorry is named *Albion* is similarly involved in this complex metaphorical web, referring us as it does to an ancient name for England but also to a more recent but perhaps equally forgotten past in which there was indeed a successful manufacturer of commercial road vehicles named Albion.

It would be possible to go through the rest of *Mercian Hymns*, providing further examples of the metaphorical complexities of the poem, but I will confine myself to one more reference, Section 25:

> Brooding on the eightieth letter of *Fors Clavigera*,
> I speak this is in memory of my grandmother, whose
> childhood and prime womanhood were spent in the
> nailer's darg.
>
> The nailshop stood back of the cottage, by the fold.
> It reeked stale mineral sweat. Sparks had furred

> its low roof. In dawn-light the troughed water
> floated a damson-bloom of dust –
>
> not to be shaken by posthumous clamour. It is one
>   thing to celebrate the 'quick forge', another
>   to cradle a face hare-lipped by the searing wire.
>
> Brooding on the eightieth letter of *Fors Clavigera*,
>   I speak this in memory of my grandmother, whose
>   childhood and prime womanhood were spent in the
>   nailer's darg.

The context for this magnificent section is set by the mention of *Fors Clavigera* (1871–8), a work by John Ruskin whose main focus was upon the glorification of manual labour. For Hill, such glorification is clearly hardly the whole of the story: indeed, it is a romanticisation of the harshness of life, as he is himself testifying in his allusions to the life of his own grandmother.

Yet, this is hardly enough; for the most extraordinary thing about this section is how the central metaphors, particularly perhaps the 'damson-bloom of dust', speak back to this idea and reconvert it. For the 'damson-bloom' is surely beautiful, or at the very least beautified by the poet; and that beauty is 'not to be shaken by posthumous clamour'. The literal reference to 'posthumous clamour' may, although we can hardly be certain of this, refer to the time after his grandmother's death; but metaphorically it seems to point us in quite a different direction from the attack on Ruskin, and to an opposite sense that this beauty, this particular kind of beauty, hard-fought and dangerous though it might be, cannot be shaken or denigrated by the thoughts or the pontifications of those who come after and who have never in fact experienced what they claim to be talking about.

It is perhaps also worth pausing for a moment on the strange word 'darg'. More common (or at least surviving in common speech until more recent times) in Scotland than in England, 'darg' is a contraction of 'day's work', and thus signifies the amount of work that can be done in a day. But here Hill is clearly putting it to a slightly different use; it would be a strange reading that did not see it as connected with the dark, the dark of the nailshop, and therefore one is reminded of the pain of this toil and simultaneously of the potential exploitation inherent in paid labour, which would constitute a further reversal of Ruskin's notions of the dignity of hard work. Not that Hill is saying that hard work is undignified: on the contrary, the 'Pieta'-like description of the cradled face brilliantly conjoins dignity and pity. But 'darg', as deployed here, expands its meaning and field of reference and comes to seem like a terrible burden, something inescapable and constraining, something opposed to all the life and vigour contained in the phrase 'girlhood and prime womanhood'.

Finally in this chapter I would like to comment on a different use of metaphor, in some stanzas from Fleur Adcock's poem 'The Ex-queen among the Astronomers' (1983):

> They serve revolving saucer eyes,
> dishes of stars; they wait upon
> huge lenses hung aloft to frame
> the slow procession of the skies.

> They calculate, adjust, record,
> watch transits, measure distances.
> They carry pocket telescopes
> to spy through when they walk abroad.

> . . .

> But she, exiled, expelled, ex-queen,
> swishes among the men of science
> waiting for cloudy skies, for nights
> when constellations can't be seen.

> She wears the rings he let her keep;
> she walks as she was taught to walk
> for his approval, years ago.
> His bitter features taunt her sleep.

> And so when these have laid aside
> their telescopes, when lids are closed
> between machine and sky, she seeks
> terrestrial bodies to bestride.

> She plucks this one or that among
> the astronomers, and is become

his canopy, his occultation;
she sucks at earlobe, penis, tongue

mouthing the tubes of flesh; her hair
crackles, her eyes are comet-sparks.
She brings the distant briefly close
above his dreamy abstract stare.

(Adcock 1983: 93)

The scenario for this beautifully patterned poem is quite clear: a queen, perhaps historical or perhaps mythical, has been exiled to a place inhabited only by the 'astronomers', who seem, perhaps, strangely reminiscent of the unworldly inhabitants of Jonathan Swift's Laputa in *Gulliver's Travels* (1726). Their concerns, therefore, are far from hers; it appears that, although in close proximity, they inhabit two different worlds. Yet, as the poem moves on, it is also as though these worlds inevitably become metaphors for each other; but then, perhaps this has been implicitly present all along. The 'revolving saucer eyes' of the very first line, for example; are these eyes through which vast distances can be seen, already being implicitly contrasted with the sharper, more present eyes of the ex-queen?

Certainly the metaphors through which the ex-queen herself is constructed take off initially from the language of the astronomers: she waits for nights 'when constellations can't be seen', so that the whole poem comes increasingly into focus, perhaps itself also a metaphorical allusion to the astronomers' telescopes, on the question of sight, of what can be seen, where, and at what distance – as it is, of course, also an extended metaphor for sexual difference. She cannot sleep, we hear; she is too ravaged by the 'bitter' events of her past; but exactly what 'lids' are closed in the sixth stanza? The lids on the telescopes and other machinery, to be sure; but also, presumably, the eyelids of the astronomers themselves, unable to make their 'calculations' when confronted with the cloudy, the dreamy, that which eludes their certainties.

And so the metaphor expands to a realm of the certain and the uncertain, considered in terms of a metaphorical opposition between the masculine and the feminine, but here with connotations that reverse conventional expectations: it is, after all, she who bestrides; it is the astronomers who possess the 'dreamy abstract stare'. It is she who becomes 'his canopy, his occultation', thus preventing him from 'focusing' on the distant, even though this does not seem to return the masculine gaze to that which, as it were, is near at hand.

And so the metaphorical structure of the poem hinges upon a lack of contact, a rejection of contact, on the incompatibility of rival perceptions of what is important and what is not. Perhaps in the end we see the ex-queen enter, if only briefly, the astronomers' world, as 'her hair/crackles, her eyes are comet-sparks'; alternatively, perhaps we are left in a state of irresolution, in a situation where the two perspectives cannot be drawn together, where distance becomes itself an apt metaphor for the relations between the genders. At all events, the tightness of the metaphorical structure allows for little respite; everything in the poem has to be in some sense translated into the terms of the other before it becomes explicable. It is true to say that, seen from one angle, the opposition between male and female perception here borders on the stereotypical; but as we have seen, it is impossible for metaphor fully to do otherwise since it relies on conventional perception, and the jarring or upsetting of that conventional perception, to achieve its effect.

10

CONCLUSION

I hope to have described so far some of the many complexities of language which begin to open out when we think about metaphor and its continual operations on the communicative stage. In order to round off this discussion, it might be appropriate to begin this conclusion with a brief set of comments on some of the metaphors writers have used to describe their own activity of writing. Here, for example, is William Congreve on the failure of inspiration or, in one of its metaphorical incarnations, 'writer's block':

> Invention flags, his Brain goes muddy,
> And black Despair succeeds brown Study.
> (Congreve 1923: IV, 160)

What is interesting here is again the nesting of metaphors one within the other. Clearly the principal metaphor is of a kind of swamp, or swamping, used to denote a condition in which nothing is clear, and also in which one is dragged down. But within this there is the phrase 'brown Study'; suitably describing the initial phase of being dragged down into the swamp or marsh when one's footsteps, like invention, 'flag', but also resonating with the notion of the study where the writer plies his craft. Words and metaphors are here, as everywhere, treacherous: taken out of context 'flags' and 'succeeds' clearly have positive connotations as much as they have negative ones. There is a further sense here of the writer's condition *vis-à-vis* the outside world, for a 'brown study' is a state in which one has lost one's awareness of one's surroundings, and is therefore all the more likely to fall into the swamp. One might be in a 'serious reverie, thoughtful absent-mindedness', to mention two definitions of the phrase; one might be in the lonely condition of the writer, as in an example given in the dictionary: 'Lack of company will soon lead a man into a brown study' (Walker 1850: 31).

These metaphors cannot be taken singularly or on their own; they are not coined, minted afresh by any particular writer; rather, they have a history, what we might term the *history of a metaphor*. Similarly with the idea of writing as some kind of consumable or comestible; as Shakespeare puts it in *Love's Labour's Lost* (1595), 'he hath never fed of the dainties that are bred in a book./He hath not eat paper, as it were, he hath not drunk ink' (Shakespeare 1990: 153). Perhaps what is most interesting about this set of metaphors is the inserted phrase, 'as it were'. 'As it were' signifies something close to the word 'like' or 'as' in a simile; all these apparently signify that we are not meant to take the text literally. But it is more complicated than this. Even if the words 'as it were' had not been there, we, the readers or watchers, would nevertheless not have taken things literally, for we know that nobody, one hopes, drinks ink; rather, the insertion of the qualifying phrase serves a communicative function; it serves to assure us that the writer is on the same side as we are, that he understands human limitations and follies with a clear eye, and is not to be taken in by the potentially overweening power of metaphor.

The image of consumption recurs in, for example, Elizabeth Gaskell's comments on all the books she has not yet read: 'I have not had time yet. But I look at them as a child looks at a cake, – with glittering eyes & watering mouth, imagining the pleasure that awaits him' (Gaskell 1966: 567). It would, then, be difficult to imagine the act of writing aside from the deployment of metaphor. To say, 'I pick up my pen and place it on the page', or to say, 'I press various keys on my keyboard', might be adequate to the physical description of writing (although even thus it would be far from complete); but the conveying of the significance of the act of constructing an imaginary world and of inviting readers into it has taxed writers down the ages. One might therefore say that at the origin of metaphor, or as one of the origins of metaphor, there lies the impossibility of conveying the act of writing itself. Writing a metaphor is thus simultaneously an act of metaphorisation of writing, without which no writer can describe his or her craft. It is the fortune and the doom of the writer to be dealing in the very materials which render the craft opaque. Seen from one angle, metaphors of writing are a series of attempts to transfer transparency onto this activity; while seen from another they merely serve to reinforce the necessary opacity of a process which is always, in some crucial sense, other than itself.

Robert Frost has more to say about this in his apposite 1931 essay 'Education by Poetry':

> [Enthusiasm] is taken through the prism of the intellect and spread on the screen in a colour, all the way from hyperbole or overstatement at one end to understatement at the other end. It is a long strip of dark lines and many colours . . . I would be willing to throw away everything else but that: enthusiasm tuned by metaphors.
>
> (Frost 1966: 36)

One of the interesting features of this comment is its dependence on synaesthesia, the replacement, translation, transference of terms from one sensory sphere to another. Here, Frost transmutes verbal activity first into the painterly ('prism', 'colour') and second into the musical ('tuned'). What, though, might it mean for 'enthusiasm' to be 'tuned' by metaphors? Here the metaphor is clearly seen not as an exercise of the wild imagination, or of Aristotelian genius, but rather the reverse, as a regulatory mechanism which provides a translation whereby the otherwise incomprehensible is rendered into some kind of harmony with what we might term the 'reading mind'.

The past two thousand years of Western tradition have seen a continuous oscillation around the notion of language and the figurative, which has paralleled a set of uncertainties over the notion of origins. This can be figured in terms of myth, as well as in ideas about writing and speech. In the current situation it is becoming increasingly clear that metaphor is a key to unlocking the structures of cultural relativity, and this has an obvious and immediate public impact in terms of, for example, the languages of prejudice and the representation of trauma. What, we might ask, will happen to metaphor next on its journey? But in asking that question, we are only repeating an adventurist, adventitious, but, alas, not very adventurous metaphor. What is important is that we insist upon an understanding that the overall notion of metaphor is no more a pre-given datum than are metaphors themselves, but is responsive to historical and linguistic development; we construct *metaphors* for our times, but we also construct *a concept of the metaphorical* for our times.

As an example of this historical process, let us consider some aspects of the evolution of the word 'shrew'. The dictionary points out to us that the shrew is a term for 'any of the small insectivorous mammals, belonging to the genus *Sorex* or the family *Soricidae*, much resembling mice but having a long sharp snout'. However, when Shakespeare wrote *The Taming of the Shrew* (1594) it was not this type of shrew he had in mind. What might be more critical is a further note in the dictionary, to the effect that 'the shrew was popularly held to be venomous and otherwise injurious'. Being a dictionary, naturally it does not go on to explore reasons why this might have been the case, but we might feel that there is something, first, in the shape of the shrew, and, second, in its smallness and rapidity of movement which may have conduced to this otherwise curious fear.

At all events, as the dictionary moves on it becomes clear that the meaning of 'shrew' intended by Shakespeare – as an uppity, uncontrollable woman, ripe for taming by a suitable man, or perhaps indeed by the whole complex force of patriarchy – is figurative, or metaphorical. There were rumours in the sixteenth century, for example, that a shrew could damage or hurt a domestic animal, obviously a deeply troubling thought in an age highly dependent on such animals economically; thus, the shrew turns into a malign force, and indeed into a figure for the Devil himself. One might reasonably wonder whether the long tail is an additional metaphorised feature here; as Chaucer puts it, 'Though that the feend noght in our sighte him shewe,/I trowe he with us be, that ilke shrewe!' (Chaucer 1912: 661).

But it is only later that this general attribution of malignancy (or perhaps it would now be better to think of it in terms of unnaturalness) becomes specifically applied to women. A classic example from 1839 is: 'He brought home with him a wife, who seemed to be a shrew, and to have the upper hand of him' (Irving 1894: 5). In this quotation we see the metaphor consolidating what was perhaps its final transformation, and becoming specifically a term of abuse to be directed at women who do not assume their supposedly correct place in a patriarchal hierarchy. The long nose of inquisitiveness, the long tail of devilry, the surreptitious and unpredictable set of movements; all have been brought together, as they partially were in Shakespeare's time, into a figure for all those traits in women which, seen from a patriarchal position, serve to undermine men's authority and men's straightforward, honourable purposes.

If we look back at Shakespeare's *The Taming of the Shrew*, it has often been critically noted that it is far from easy to determine the level of irony in the play. To put it very crudely, does the play support a view that women who get beyond their assigned station are to be tamed? Or does it say that women in such a position are in fact unhappy, and that therefore their taming is somehow conducive to their own well-being, as well as to the well-being of a properly ordered society? Or is Shakespeare at least partly mocking the pretensions of those foolish men who believe that such taming can actually be effective or productive? The force of the metaphor is so strong that it makes these questions difficult to answer. Although metaphors may appear to offer a certain precision, in the sense we have already mentioned of a translation from that which is difficult to describe to something which is more 'familiar', in another sense metaphor is opaque; it conjoins dissimilars, not always for the purposes of enlightenment but sometimes in order to prevent or deflect criticism of unthought assumptions.

'To shrew', a verb now obsolete, was in the later Middle Ages and for some time afterwards a synonym for 'to curse', or to cast the evil eye; it is hard to evade the possibility that there are suggestions of witchcraft in this collocation. Thus, a small animal and one which is harmless, except of course to insects, cuts, as it were, a figure in the world; it becomes taken up and put through a series of historical and textual transmutations which end with the image of the overweening, displaced woman. Or rather, we should add, *did* end there, since the term 'shrew' in any of these meanings is hardly any more in common use, partly because more violent protestations of frightened male dominance such as 'bitch' and 'cow' have become more prevalent.

Thus, again, we need to see metaphor not only as something which is made or constructed by, for example, particular literary writers, but also as something inherited, something unexamined, something belonging to the cultural unconscious. And all this without examining the complex connections between the shrew and that word which is still in common currency, 'shrewd', which, as we might by now expect, derives from the same source, and bore the metaphorical weight of malignancy and cunning long before it became rehabilitated, albeit in a somewhat ambiguous way, to refer to cleverness and insight.

However, in order to complete our summary of the complexities of metaphor, it is necessary to return to deconstruction, and especially to the specific succession within deconstruction between Martin Heidegger and Jacques Derrida. In his masterly book *Derrida, Heidegger, Blanchot* (1992) Timothy Clark quotes a significant passage from Derrida's essay 'The Retrait of Metaphor' (1978a) on what he refers to as the 'doubling of metaphor':

> As this withdrawal of the metaphoric leaves no place free for a discourse of the proper or the literal it will have at the same time the sense of a re-fold (*re-pli*), of what retreats like a wave on the shoreline, and of a re-turn (*re-tour*), of the overcharging repetition of a supplementary trait, of yet another metaphor, of a double trait (*re-trait*) of metaphor, a discourse whose rhetorical border is no longer determinable according to a simple and indivisible line, according to a linear and indecomposable trait.
>
> (Clark 1992: 119)

This may seem at first glance a characteristically difficult and complicated passage of Derrida's, but the thinking behind it is really quite simple. Essentially, if I may dare to use such a term, Derrida is saying that no attempt to *isolate* metaphor as part of a poetic practice or as part of a critical activity can be truly successful; the processes of metaphor are already deeply twined around the evolution of language and around the rhetorical skills, unconscious or otherwise, which we need to learn to acquire in order to be able to communicate with each other. The image of the shoreline might remind us of a similar image, in Iain Banks's novel *The Bridge*, an image based on classical sources, of a man whose destiny appears to be to beat at the waves with a flail.

This, obviously, is not a particularly useful activity; it perhaps bears comparison with the sad hopes of the Walrus in Lewis Carroll's 'The Walrus and the Carpenter' (1872) concerning the possibility of counting the grains of sand on a beach. For all will be disturbed by, among other things, the thought of 'what retreats like a wave on the shoreline'. I read this metaphor of Derrida's in several different ways. First, the 'wave' itself disappears; it is no longer there. Similarly, the operation of metaphor, at least in one sense, leaves no visible trace; metaphor comes and goes, it moves towards the margin, the verge of intelligibility, and then again it retreats. But second, despite this apparent evanescence, it is of the utmost power: not only the sand but also the rocks and cliffs that constitute the shoreline have, in the end, been mainly formed by the waves, which even now possess the power to crumble whole shorelines into dust and, as we are increasingly appreciating in the aftermath of modernity's worship of the god of development, similarly to obliterate whole island nations. So there is in metaphor an uncanny combination of evanescence and permanence, of power and vulnerability, of resistance to change and the spread of change.

But third, in the Derrida passage, one can point to what might be called the sinister power, the left-handed power, of metaphor, which 'leaves no place free for a discourse of the proper or the literal'. It is not that the world of language is neatly divided into two provinces of the literal and the metaphorical, any more than we can say that the Earth is divided into two provinces of the land and the sea. Geologically these formations only arise or indeed submerge as a result of complex and unending interactions with one another. Who can say where the sea ends and the land begins, or vice versa? It is perhaps interesting that, at least in the British context, the shoreline is Crown property. We may construe this in several ways: as a demonstration of monarchical power, as the necessity of maintaining central control over the marginal, but also, surely, as a way of maintaining some kind of national boundary precisely at that point where the very notion of a stable boundary is most under threat.

We might in this context consider, or perhaps reconsider, T.S. Eliot's well-known lines in 'East Coker':

> each venture
> Is a new beginning, a raid on the inarticulate
> With shabby equipment always deteriorating
> In the general mess of imprecision of feeling
> (Eliot 1963: 203)

'East Coker' was written, probably, in 1940, and thus it is unsurprising to find Eliot using military metaphors like the 'raid' and the 'shabby equipment'. It is, however, open to the reader to decide quite what weight to place on the 'general mess', a phrase which in time of war might have unconsciously extended the obvious meaning of 'general' to include the role of a military commander, and the meaning of 'mess' to include the common military description of the place where soldiers eat. The point, though, would be to figure the process of organising language ('I gotta use words when I talk to you') as one where there is an inevitability about a sequence of successes and failures 'where ignorant armies clash by night' (Arnold 1950: 212), to quote Matthew Arnold. The successful, and by implication metaphorical, use of language then becomes a series of manoeuvres; and perhaps even more to the point, the humble practitioners of language, which includes all of us, are rarely in a position ourselves to declare whether these 'raids' have been successful or unsuccessful. What remains certain, if anything does, is that the shoreline *will* remain the same, according to some kind of timescale, but it will also *never* be the same from day to day, from minute to minute, as suitable metaphors are cast and recast, forged and reforged, always under the pressure of what might seem intelligible from the shore, but always difficult to perceive at the time of, for example, what W.S. Graham refers to as the 'night bell' (Graham 2004: 105), which summons us to the shoreline but always under conditions of obscurity and uncertainty.

A little later in his book, Clark comments that: 'What is ineluctable is not primarily language commonly conceived as representation, mirroring a realm of objects, nor yet language as presentation, rather, as it were, a mirror that *faces inward* in the re-mark' (Clark 1992: 123). This kind of phrasing might fairly remind us of J.H. Prynne's wrestling with language, almost as though the 're-mark', the moment when, as I interpret it, language makes *its own* statement, comes into clear focus. This statement will have at most an oblique relation to the statement we might have thought we were making when we dreamt of the forever receding possibility of using it. It turns to face us with a declaration, one which is always uncanny, always half in twilight, that the perennial attempt to rid language of its ambiguities is doomed and perhaps weirdly counterproductive, an attempt again to draw that notorious metaphor, a 'line in the sand'.

If I may venture a final metaphorical interpretation: mirrors are made of sand. The apparently clear glass of language as classically conceived is composed out of the most opaque of media – precisely that sand which, according to E.T.A. Hoffmann (1979), Freud and the various folkloric originators of their respective narratives, when rubbed into the eyes robs the possessor of those eyes of sight, understanding and eventually, perhaps, of the eyes themselves. We are therefore reminded of whatever those eyes might signify in psychoanalytical terms of the mastery of difficult and confusing materials. The cumulative metaphors of Western civilisation are certainly based on sight, as we have seen; but equally they are based on the terror of a blindness which would place us in a night, on a tremulous shoreline, where our other senses, vestiges and atrophies as they are, would be of little avail.

What, then, is metaphor? The suggestions I have tried to offer in this book, and the examples I have provided, point to the fact that there is no single, universal, ahistorical definition of 'metaphor'. Metaphor is what metaphor has been taken to be at various times and in various cultures. Nevertheless, we cannot leave the concept in this unsatisfactory condition. We can say that the term 'metaphor' has usually been used to denote a peculiarity, or perhaps better an innate property, of language. This property is one of constant excess or dissemination. The simplest of words ('head', 'home', 'animal') have metaphorical ramifications which cannot be simply denied or evaded, although it is possible, to a limited extent, to select among them in a contextual way. Metaphor is perhaps the principal sign that words do not stand in isolation; so long as they have histories – and all words do, even ones that appear newly coined – then they will have a metaphorical field of their own. I return again to the newspaper, where I happen today to read (not, I suspect, for the first time): 'Belfast sighs as peace deal slips away again'. Of course, Belfast does not sigh; a city cannot sigh any more than it can sleep, or rejoice, or do any of the other anthropomorphic things that newspaper headlines would have it do. It is possible that the people within it may sigh, although it is unlikely that they would all do so at the same time; and that would be a prime example of metonymy, the process whereby an interchange occurs between the whole and the part, between Belfast and its human inhabitants. But the 'sigh of Belfast' here is a metaphor; it is a metaphor for a state of mind, but even to say that is too simple, for whose state of mind is this? Belfast, it says; but might one not equally say that this 'sigh' is at least in part the presumed reaction of the reader of the newspaper, the observer of the scene of defeat of hope? The hope of a peace deal 'slips away'; again, not literally, but perhaps this image confronts us more starkly with the problem of metaphor, because the metaphor of something slipping away, something which might be a hope, a relationship, a life, is so closely embedded within the language that it is difficult, if not impossible, to perceive its metaphoric force.

Glossary

Allegory A work of literature, usually in the form of a substantial narrative, in which more than one chain of meanings can be discerned; the most obvious example in English literature is John Bunyan's *Pilgrim's Progress*, where the surface story is accompanied by a set of deeper, Christian references.

Amalgamated metaphor A metaphor which mixes different realms of discourse, sometimes accidentally, at other times for comic effect.

Anthropomorphism A device whereby human attributes are granted to that which is not human, ranging from the humanising of a deity, as so often in Greek myth, to the humanising of animals, other aspects of the natural world, and even man-made objects.

Conceit The conceit is often regarded as typical of metaphysical poetry. As a use of metaphor, it is distinguished first by the apparent initial dissonance between the two terms of comparison, and second by its sustenance over considerable length, sometimes the length of an entire poem.

Dead metaphor A metaphor which has been used so often that it barely stands out as a metaphor at all and has descended to the level of cliché. Typical of much political language.

Extended metaphor A metaphor extended and developed throughout a text, or throughout significant portions of it. Sometimes this can produce a certain gravity; sometimes, as for example often in the works of Jonathan Swift, a certain levity.

Homonym Words which, although spelt identically, derive from different origins. An example would be 'stang', which is a past-tense form of the verb 'to sting' but also a noun meaning a pole or bar.

Image This is one of the most frequently used words in literary criticism, and over time its meanings have become exceptionally diffuse. Originally related to the possibilities of making 'pictures in words', it has since been extended to cover almost all uses of figurative (non-literal) language, and thus to become a term almost as wide as 'literature' itself, as distinguished from, for example, instruction manuals; although some would claim that even instruction manuals have in some sense to do with the imagistic, both in their use of actual images and in their attempt to express one discursive realm in terms of another.

Latent meaning/Manifest meaning Two terms which derive from Freudian psychoanalysis, and especially from Freud's work on the nature of dreams. The 'manifest meaning' refers to the apparent signification of the dream – the images we remember; the latent meaning can be uncovered only by analytical reflection on these images, and by the attempt to relate them to aspects of our past life, and especially our childhood.

Metonymy This occurs in many forms, but it is essentially a process of substitution, whereby the reader is brought to understanding not by full relation but by the realisation of, often, a small part which stands in for the whole. One might think, for example, of 'bricks and mortar', a phrase which stands in for the whole realm of buildings, of real estate, and indeed, at a wider level, for a concept of financial security.

Mixed metaphor This is a metaphor which mixes apparently incompatible topics. It is often the result of a rhetorical mistake but sometimes – in, for example, the works of the US poet Ogden Nash – it may be used to remarkable effect.

Recuperation The force of this term depends on the idea that literature is essentially strange, it unsettles and troubles our ideas of the world. A recuperative narrative is one which, despite this, goes in for a 'happy ending'. Recuperative criticism is criticism which affirms the 'wholeness' of a work of art, even when that work might be fractured, challenging, incomplete.

Simile A form of metaphor, often regarded as the simplest of all, where the comparison between two objects is expressed through the link words 'like' or 'as'. Most more advanced forms of metaphor seek to surprise and startle by omitting these link words.

Subject(ivity) This immensely complex word has been the focus of much of the critical activity of recent times. The principal focus has been on the ambiguity, or even paradox, contained in the word, since, on the one hand, it signifies authority ('I am the subject of this conversation') while, on the other, it signifies reduction, powerlessness ('I am being subjected to a great deal of gossip'). Subjectivity supposes that we have individual, independent opinions and perspectives; a great deal of modern critical theory challenges this and suggests that we are instead 'subjected' to opinions expressed by others in, for example, the tabloid press.

Synaesthesia The representation of one sense in terms of another; or the melding of the senses so that we become uncertain as to which sense is being referred to.

Synecdoche The substitution of a part for a whole, as in the example of 'twenty head' for 'twenty cows'.

Tenor/Vehicle According to some literary theories, these are useful terms in which to describe the two 'parts' of a metaphor, the tenor being the term which is being represented, the vehicle being the term which is doing the representing. In Robert Burns's phrase 'My love is like a red red rose', the rose would be the vehicle representing the tenor of love.

BIBLIOGRAPHY

Abse, Dannie, *Collected Poems 1948–1976* (London: Hutchinson, 1977)

Achebe, Chinua, *Things Fall Apart* (London: Heinemann, 1958)

Adcock, Fleur, *Selected Poems* (Oxford: Oxford University Press, 1983)

Alexiou, Margaret, *After Antiquity: Greek Language, Myth and Metaphor* (Ithaca, NY: Cornell University Press, 2002)

Allen, Sture (ed.), *Nobel Lectures in Literature 1968–80* (Singapore: World Scientific Publishing, 1993)

Althusser, Louis, *Lenin and Philosophy and Other Essays*, trans. Ben Brewster (2nd edn, London: NLB, 1977)

Anon., *Sir Gawain and the Green Knight*, ed. and introd. W.R.J. Baron (Manchester: Manchester University Press, 1998)

Anzieu, Didier, *The Skin Ego*, trans. Chris Turner (New Haven, CN: Yale University Press, 1989)

Aristotle, *The Poetics*, ed. and trans. Stephen Halliwell, with Longinus, *On the Sublime*, trans. W.H. Fyfe, and Demetrius, *On Style*, ed. and trans. Doreen C. Innes (Cambridge, MA: Harvard University Press, 1909)

Arnold, Matthew, *Poetical Works*, ed. C.B. Tinker and H.F. Lowry (London: Oxford University Press, 1950)

Avis, Paul, *God and the Creative Imagination: Metaphor, Symbol and Myth in Religion and Theology* (London: Routledge, 1999)

Banks, Iain, *The Bridge* (London: Macmillan, 1986)

Barthelme, Donald, *Snow White* (New York: Prentice-Hall and IBD, 1996)

Barthes, Roland, *Mythologies*, trans. Annette Lavers (St Albans: Granada, 1973)

—— *Image/Music/Text: Essays*, trans. Stephen Heath (London: Fontana, 1977)

Beckett, Samuel, *Murphy* (London: Pan, 1973)

—— *Waiting for Godot*, ed. David Bradby (Cambridge: Cambridge University Press, 2001)

Bickerstaffe, Isaac, *et al.*, *A Volume of Farces as they are Performed at the Theatre, Smoke-Alley, Dublin* (Dublin: 1792)

Black, Max, *Models and Metaphors: Studies in Language and Philosophy* (Ithaca, NY: Cornell University Press, 1962)

Blake, William, *Complete Writings*, ed. Geoffrey Keynes (London: Oxford University Press, 1966)

Boehmer, Elleke, *Colonial and Postcolonial Literature: Migrant Metaphors* (2nd edn, Oxford: Oxford University Press, 2005)

Boys-Stones, G.R. (ed.), *Metaphor, Allegory and the Classical Tradition: Ancient Thought and Modern Revisions* (Oxford: Oxford University Press, 2003)

Brontë, Charlotte, *Jane Eyre*, ed. Q.D. Leavis (Harmondsworth: Penguin, 1966)

Brooke-Rose, Christine, *A Grammar of Metaphor* (London: Secker and Warburg, 1958)

Bunyan, John, *The Pilgrim's Progress*, ed. W.R. Owens (Oxford: Oxford University Press, 2003)

Burns, Robert, *The Canongate Burns*, introd. Andrew Noble, ed. Andrew Noble and Patrick Scott Hogg (Edinburgh: Canongate, 2001)

Cameron, Lynne, and Graham Low (eds), *Researching and Applying Metaphor* (Cambridge: Cambridge University Press, 1999)

Carroll, Lewis, *The Complete Works* (London: CRW, 2005)

Chaucer, Geoffrey, *The Complete Works*, ed. Walter W. Skeat (London: Oxford University Press, 1912)

Clark, Timothy, *Derrida, Heidegger, Blanchot* (Cambridge: Cambridge University Press, 1992)

Coetzee, J.M., *Waiting for the Barbarians* (London: Secker and Warburg, 1980)

Coleridge, Samuel Taylor, *Biographia Literaria*, ed. George Watson (London: J.M. Dent, 1956)

—— *Poetical Works*, ed. Ernest Hartley Coleridge (London: Oxford University Press, 1967)

—— *Table Talk*, ed. Carl Woodring (2 vols, London: Routledge, 1990)

Collins, Wilkie, *The Woman in White*, ed. Harvey Peter Sucksmith (London: Oxford University Press, 1975)

Congreve, William, *The Complete Works*, ed. Montague Summers (4 vols, Soho: Nonesuch Press, 1923)

Conrad, Joseph, *Heart of Darkness*, ed. Paul O'Prey (London: Penguin, 1983)

—— *Under Western Eyes* (London: Dent, 1991)

Cooper, David E., *Metaphor* (Oxford: Blackwell, 1986)

Dante Alighieri, *The Inferno*, trans. Ciaran Carson (London: Granta, 2002)

Deleuze, Gilles and Félix Guattari, *A Thousand Plateaus: Capitalism and Schizophrenia*, trans. Brian Massumi (London: Athlone Press, 1988)

Derrida, Jacques, *Of Grammatology*, trans. Gayatri Chakravorty Spivak (Baltimore, MD: Johns Hopkins University Press, 1976)

—— 'The Retrait of Metaphor', trans. F. Gasdner *et al.*, *Enclitic* 2, 2, pp. 5–33 (1978a)

—— *Writing and Difference*, trans. and introd. Alan Bass (London: Routledge and Kegan Paul, 1978b)

Dickens, Charles, *The Mystery of Edwin Drood*, ed. Arthur J. Cox, introd. Angus Wilson (London: Penguin, 1974)

Donne, John, *Poems*, ed. John Carey (Oxford: Oxford University Press, 1990)

Draaisma, Douwe, *Metaphors of Memory: A History of Ideas about the Mind*, trans. Paul Vincent (Cambridge: Cambridge University Press, 2000)

Dryden, John, *Essays*, ed. W.P. Ker (Oxford: Clarendon, 1926)

Dunn, Douglas, *Selected Poems 1964–1983* (London: Faber and Faber, 1986)

Dylan, Bob, *Lyrics 1962–1985* (London: HarperCollins, 1994)

Ekstroem, M.S., *Illusion, Lie and Metaphor: The Paradox of Divergence in Early Chinese Poetics* [abstract] (Durham, NC: Duke University Press, 2002)

Eliot, T.S., *Collected Poems 1909–1962* (London: Faber and Faber, 1963)

Equiano, Olaudah, *The Interesting Life and Other Writings*, ed. and introd. Vincent Carretta (London: Penguin, 2003)

Fernandez, James W. (ed.), *Beyond Metaphor: The Theory of Tropes in Anthropology* (Stanford, CA: Stanford University Press, 1991)

Fish, Stanley, *Is There a Text in this Class?: The Authority of Interpretive Communities* (Cambridge, MA: Harvard University Press, 1980)

Fisher, Roy, *Poems 1955–1980* (Oxford: Oxford University Press, 1980)

Flecker, James Elroy, *The Collected Poems*, ed. and introd. J.C. Squire (London: Martin Secker, 1916)

Fleming, Ian, *Dr No* (London: Pan, 1958)

Forster, E.M., *A Passage to India* (London: David Campbell, 1991)

Fowles, John, *The French Lieutenant's Woman* (London: Jonathan Cape, 1969)

Freud, Sigmund, 'The Uncanny', in *The Standard Edition of the Complete Psychological Works of Sigmund Freud*, ed. James Strachey *et al.* (24 vols, London: The Hogarth Press and the Institute of Psycho-analysis, 1953–74), Vol. XVII (1955)

—— *The Interpretation of Dreams*, in *The Standard Edition of the Complete Psychological Works of Sigmund Freud*, ed. James Strachey *et al.* (24 vols, London: The Hogarth Press and the Institute of Psycho-analysis, 1953–74), Vols IV and V (1958)

—— *Jokes and their Relation to the Unconscious*, in *The Standard Edition of the Complete Psychological Works of Sigmund Freud*, ed. James Strachey *et al.* (24 vols, London: The Hogarth Press and the Institute of Psycho-analysis, 1953–74), Vol. VIII (1960)

—— *Civilisation and its Discontents*, in *The Standard Edition of the Complete Psychological Works of Sigmund Freud*, ed. James Strachey *et al.* (24 vols, London: The Hogarth Press and the Institute of Psycho-analysis, 1953–74), Vol. XXI (1964)

Frost, Robert, *Selected Prose*, ed. Hyde Cox and Edward Connery Lathem (New York: Holt, 1966)

Frye, Northrop, *Myth and Metaphor: Selected Essays 1974–1988*, ed. Robert D. Denham (Charlottesville: University Press of Virginia, 1990)

Fussell, Edwin, *Lucifer in Harness: American Metre, Metaphor and Diction* (Princeton, NJ: Princeton University Press, 1973)

Gaskell, Elizabeth, *The Letters of Mrs Gaskell*, ed. J.A.V. Chapple and Arthur Pollard (Manchester: Manchester University Press, 1966)

Gibbons, David, *Metaphor in Dante* (Oxford: Legenda, 2002)

Gibson, William, *Neuromancer* (London: Victor Gollancz, 1984)

—— *Pattern Recognition* (New York: G.P. Putnam's Sons, 2003)

Goatly, Andrew, *The Language of Metaphors: An Introduction* (London: Routledge, 1996)

Graham, W.S., *New Collected Poems*, ed. Matthew Francis (London: Faber and Faber, 2004)

Gray, Martin, *A Dictionary of Literary Terms* (2nd edn, London: Longman York Press, 1992)

Greene, Graham, *Brighton Rock* (Harmondsworth: Penguin, 1970)

Guttenplan, Samuel, *Objects of Metaphor* (Oxford: Clarendon Press, 2005)

Hardy, Thomas, *The Complete Poems*, ed. James Gibson (London: Palgrave, 2001)

Harrison, Stephen, Michael Paschalis and Stavros Frangoulidis (eds), *Metaphor and the Ancient Novel* (Groningen: Barkhuis, 2005)

Hausman, Carl R., *Metaphor and Art: Interactionism and Reference in the Verbal and Nonverbal Arts* (Cambridge: Cambridge University Press, 1989)

Hester, Marcus B., *The Meaning of Metaphor: An Analysis in the Light of Wittgenstein's Claim that Meaning is Use* (The Hague and Paris: Mouton, 1967)

Hill, Geoffrey, *Mercian Hymns* (London: André Deutsch, 1971)

Hillman, James, *The Dream and the Underworld* (New York: Harper and Row, 1979)

Hoban, Russell, *The Moment under the Moment* (London: Jonathan Cape, 1962)

Hoffmann, E.T.A., *The Best Tales of E.T.A. Hoffmann*, ed. E.F. Bleiler (New York: Dover, 1979)

Hopkins, Gerard Manley, *The Poetical Works*, ed. Norman H. Mackenzie (Oxford: Clarendon Press, 1990)

Hughes, Ted, *Selected Poems 1957–1981* (London: Faber and Faber, 1982)

Huxley, Aldous, *Brave New World*, introd. David Bradshaw (London: Flamingo, 1994)

Inge, William Ralph, *Outspoken Essays (First Series)* (London: Longmans, Green and Co., 1919)

Ionesco, Eugène, *Rhinoceros, The Chairs, The Lesson*, trans. Donald Watson (Harmondsworth: Penguin, 1962)

Irving, Washington, *Wolfert's Roost*, with *Adventures of Captain Bonneville* (London: George Bell and Sons, 1894)

Johnson, Mark, *Metaphor and Philosophy* (Mahwah, NJ: Lawrence Erlbaum, 1995)

Jonson, Ben, *Poems*, ed. Ian Donaldson (London: Oxford University Press, 1975)

Kael, Pauline, *The Citizen Kane Book* (London: Secker and Warburg, 1971)

Kafka, Franz, *Metamorphosis and Other Stories*, trans. Willa Muir and Edwin Muir (Harmondsworth: Penguin, 1961)

Kittay, Eva Feder, *Metaphor: Its Cognitive Force and Linguistic Structure* (Oxford: Clarendon, 1987)

Knapp, Bettina L., *Machine, Metaphor and the Writer: A Jungian View* (University Park: Pennsylvania State University Press, 1989)

Knights, L.C., and Basil Cottle (eds), *Metaphor and Symbol* (London: Butterworths, 1960)

Knowles, Murray, and Rosamund Moon, *Introducing Metaphor* (London: Routledge, 2006)

Kreitman, Norman, *The Roots of Metaphor: A Multidisciplinary Study in Aesthetics* (Aldershot: Ashgate, 1999)

Lakoff, George, and Mark Johnson, *Metaphors We Live By* (Chicago, IL: Chicago University Press, 1980)

Lakoff, George, and Mark Turner, *More than Cool Reason: A Field Guide to Poetic Metaphor* (Chicago, IL: Chicago University Press, 1989)

Larkin, Philip, *Collected Poems*, ed. Anthony Thwaite (London: The Marvell Press and Faber and Faber, 1988)

Lear, Edward, *The Complete Nonsense of Edward Lear*, ed. and introd. Holbrook Jackson (London: Faber and Faber, 1947)

Leary, David E. (ed.), *Metaphors in the History of Psychology* (Cambridge: Cambridge University Press, 1990)

Leatherdale, W.H., *The Role of Analogy, Model and Metaphor in Science* (New York: Elsevier, 1974)

Leino, Anna-Liisa, and Margareth Drakenberg, *Metaphor: An Educational Perspective* (Helsinki: University of Helsinki Press, 1993)

Lessing, Doris, *Canopus in Argos: Archives* (London: Vintage, 1992)

Levin, Samuel R., *The Semantics of Metaphor* (Baltimore, MD: The Johns Hopkins University Press, 1977)

Lodge, David, *Changing Places: A Tale of Two Campuses* (London: Secker and Warburg, 1975)

—— *The Modes of Modern Writing: Metaphor, Metonymy and the Typology of Modern Literature* (London: Edward Arnold, 1977)

Lopez, José, *Society and its Metaphors: Language, Social Theory and Social Structure* (New York and London: Continuum, 2003)

MacBeth, George, with Edward Lucie-Smith and Jack Clemo, *Penguin Modern Poets 6* (Harmondsworth: Penguin, 1964)

Marks, Lawrence E., Robin J. Hammeal and Marc H. Bornstein, *Perceiving Similarity and Comprehending Metaphor* (Chicago, IL: Chicago University Press, 1987)

Martell, Yann, *Life of Pi* (Edinburgh: Canongate, 2002)

McCarthy, Cormac, *The Border Trilogy* (London: Pan Macmillan, 2002)

McFague, Sallie, *Speaking in Parables: A Study in Metaphor and Theology* (London: SCM, 1975)

Melville, Herman, *Moby-Dick*, ed. Hershel Parker and Harrison Hayford (2nd edn, New York: Norton, 2001)

Milton, John, *The Complete Poems*, ed. B.A. Wright, introd. Gordon Campbell (London: Dent, 1980)

Mooij, Jan Johann, *A Study of Metaphor: On the Nature of Metaphorical Expressions* (Amsterdam: North Holland, 1976)

Morgan, Edwin, *Selected Poems* (Manchester: Carcanet, 1985)

Murray, Les, *Killing the Black Dog: Essays and Poems* (Annandale, NSW: Federation Press, 1997)

Newbolt, Henry, *Collected Poems 1897–1907* (London: Nelson, 1907)

Nicolson, Harold, *Diaries and Letters 3, 1945–1962*, ed. Nigel Nicolson (London: Collins, 1968)

Olney, James, *Metaphors of Self and the Meaning of Autobiography* (Princeton, NJ: Princeton University Press, 1972)

Ortony, Andrew (ed.), *Metaphor and Thought* (Cambridge: Cambridge University Press, 1979)

Orwell, George, *The Lion and the Unicorn: Socialism and the English Genius* (London: Secker and Warburg, 1941)

—— *1984*, ed. Peter Davison and Ben Pimlott (London: Penguin, 1989)

Owen, Stephen (ed. and trans.), *An Anthology of Chinese Literature: Beginnings to 1911* (London and New York: W.W. Norton, 1996)

Peake, Mervyn, *Gormenghast* (London: Eyre and Spottiswoode, 1950)

Piozzi, Hester Lynch, *Anecdotes of the Late Samuel Johnson, during the Last Twenty Years of his Life*, ed. S.C. Roberts (Cambridge: Cambridge University Press, 1925)

Plath, Sylvia, *Collected Poems*, ed. and introd. Ted Hughes (London: Faber and Faber, 1981)

Poe, Edgar Allan, *Selected Tales*, ed. David van Leer (Oxford: Oxford University Press, 1998)

Pope, Alexander, *Poetical Works*, ed. Herbert Davis (London: Oxford University Press, 1966)

Pratchett, Terry, *Guards! Guards!* (London: Victor Gollancz, 1989)

Prynne, Jeremy, *Poems* (2nd edn, Tarset: Bloodaxe, 2005)

Raban, Jonathan, *Passage to Juneau: A Sea and its Meanings* (New York: Vintage, 2000)

Radcliffe, Ann, *The Castles of Athlin and Dunbayne*, ed. Alison Milbank (Oxford: Oxford University Press, 1995)

Rehder, Robert, *Stevens, Williams, Crane and the Motive for Metaphor* (Basingstoke: Palgrave Macmillan, 2004)

Rhys, Jean, *Wide Sargasso Sea* (Harmondsworth: Penguin, 1997)

Ricoeur, Paul, *The Rule of Metaphor: Multi-disciplinary Studies of the Creation of Meaning in Language*, trans. Robert Czerny, Kathleen McLaughlin and John Costello (London: Routledge and Kegan Paul, 1978)

Rothbart, Daniel, *Explaining the Growth of Scientific Knowledge: Metaphors, Models and Meanings* (Lewiston, Queenston, Lampeter: Edwin Mellen Press, 1997)

Royle, Nicholas, *Telepathy and Literature: Essays on the Reading Mind* (Oxford: Blackwell, 1990)

—— *The Uncanny* (Manchester: Manchester University Press, 2003)

Rushdie, Salman, *Midnight's Children* (London: Jonathan Cape, 1981)

—— *The Ground beneath her Feet* (London: Jonathan Cape, 1999)

Sacks, Sheldon (ed.), *On Metaphor* (Chicago, IL: University of Chicago Press, 1979)

Scheffler, Israel, *Beyond the Letter: A Philosophical Enquiry into Ambiguity, Vagueness and Metaphor in Language* (London: Routledge and Kegan Paul, 1979)

Shakespeare, William, *Hamlet*, ed. Edward Hubler (New York: Penguin, 1963)

—— *Love's Labour's Lost*, ed. G.R. Hibbard (Oxford: Oxford University Press, 1990)

—— *The Taming of the Shrew*, ed. Ann Thompson (Cambridge: Cambridge University Press, 2003)

Shibles, Warren A., *Metaphor: An Annotated Bibliography and History* (Whitewater, WI: Language Press, 1971)

Soskice, Janet Martin, *Metaphor and Religious Language* (Oxford: Clarendon Press, 1985)

Spenser, Edmund, *The Faerie Queene*, ed. A.C. Hamilton (London: Longman, 2001)

Spitzer, Michael, *Metaphor and Musical Thought* (Chicago, IL: Chicago University Press, 2004)

Stanford, W.B., *Greek Metaphor: Studies in Theory and Practice* (Oxford: Blackwell, 1936)

Stern, Josef, *Metaphor in Context* (Cambridge, MA: MIT Press, 2000)

Sternberg, Robert J., *Metaphors of Mind: Conceptions of the Nature of Intelligence* (Cambridge: Cambridge University Press, 1990)

Stitt, Megan Perigoe, *Metaphors of Change in the Language of Nineteenth-Century Fiction: Scott, Gaskell and Kingsley* (Oxford: Clarendon Press, 1998)

Swift, Jonathan, *Gulliver's Travels* (London: Dent, 1991)

Tennyson, Alfred Lord, *A Selected Edition*, ed. Christopher Ricks (London: Longman, 1969)

Tilley, Christopher, *Metaphor and Material Culture* (Oxford: Blackwell, 1999)

Tolkien, J.R.R., *Lord of the Rings* (New York and London: HarperCollins, 2005)

Turner, Victor, *Dramas, Fields and Metaphors: Symbolic Action in Human Society* (Ithaca, NY: Cornell University Press, 1974)

Tutuola, Amos, *The Palm-Wine Drinkard, and his dead Palm-Wine Tapster in the Deads' Town* (London: Faber and Faber, 1952)

Van Norden, Bryan W., review of *Comparative Essays in Early Greek and Chinese Rational Thinking*, ed. Jean-Paul Reding, *Notre Dame Philosophical Reviews* (2004)

Walcott, Derek, *Collected Poems 1948–1984* (London: Faber and Faber, 1992)

Walker, Gilbert, *A Manifest Detection of the Most Vyle and Detestable Use of Dice-Play* (London: Percy Society, 1850)

Walpole, Horace, *The Castle of Otranto*, ed. W.S. Lewis (London: Oxford University Press, 1969)

Wheelwright, Philip, *Metaphor and Reality* (Bloomington: Indiana University Press, 1962)

White, Roger M., *The Structure of Metaphor: The Way the Language of Metaphor Works* (Oxford: Blackwell, 1996)

Whittock, Trevor, *Metaphor and Film* (Cambridge: Cambridge University Press, 1990)

Whitworth, Michael H., *Einstein's Wake: Relativity, Metaphor and Modernist Literature* (Oxford: Oxford University Press, 2002)

Wilkinson, P.R., *Thesaurus of Traditional English Metaphors* (London and New York: Routledge, 1993)

Williamson, Judith, *Decoding Advertisements: Ideology and Meaning in Advertising* (London: Boyars, 1978)

Wordsworth, William, and Samuel Taylor Coleridge, *Lyrical Ballads*, ed. R.L. Brett and A.L. Jones (London: Methuen, 1968)

Yeats, W.B., *Collected Poems* (London: Macmillan, 1965)

Young, Robert M., *Darwin's Metaphor: Nature's Place in Victorian Culture* (Cambridge: Cambridge University Press, 1985)

Zon, Bennett, *Music and Metaphor in Nineteenth-Century British Musicology* (Aldershot: Ashgate, 2000)

Index

The Routledge Dictionary of Literary Terms
Peter Childs and Roger Fowler

The Routledge Dictionary of Literary Terms is a twenty-first century update of Roger Fowler's seminal *Dictionary of Modern Critical Terms*. Bringing together original entries written by such celebrated theorists as Terry Eagleton and Malcolm Bradbury with new definitions of current terms and controversies, this is the essential reference book for students of literature at all levels. This book includes:

- New definitions of contemporary critical issues such as 'Cybercriticism' and 'Globalization'.
- An exhaustive range of entries, covering numerous aspects to such topics as genre, form, cultural theory and literary technique.
- Complete coverage of traditional and radical approaches to the study and production of literature.
- Thorough account of critical terminology and analyses of key academic debates.
- Full cross-referencing throughout and suggestions for further reading.

Hbk: 978-0-415-36117-0
Pbk: 978-0-415-34017-5
Ebk: 978-0-203-46291-1

Available at all good bookshops
For ordering and further information please visit
www.routledge.com

Related titles from Routledge

Doing English
A Guide for Literature Students
Robert Eaglestone

Aimed at students in the final year of secondary education, on Access courses or beginning degrees, this immensely readable book provides the ideal introduction to studying English. It will:

- orient you, by explaining what you are doing when you are studying literature
- equip you, by explaining key current ideas about English and literature
- help you to bridge the gap from secondary to higher education, by showing how and why English is changing and by introducing the study of literary theory.

Doing English examines the evolution of English as a subject and questions the assumptions that lie behind approaches to literature. The author deals with the exciting new ideas and contentious debates that make up English today, covering a range of issues from critical approaches to value, the canon and Shakespeare, to cultural heritage and national identity and on to the future of English. This volume is an essential purchase for all those planning to 'do' English.

Hbk: 978-0-415-28422-6
Pbk: 978-0-415-28423-3

Available at all good bookshops
For ordering and further information please visit:
www.routledge.com

Related titles from Routledge

Introducing Metaphor
By Murray Knowles and Rosamund Moon

'A valuable and enlightening contribution . . . an excellent introductory textbook to metaphor studies, accessible both to people
who are being introduced to the study of metaphor for the very
first time and to people well-versed in metaphor studies . . . this
book is strongly recommended ... it is a real contribution to
metaphor studies.' – *The Linguist List*

Filling a distinct gap in introductory literature, this accessible guide to the
theory and applications of metaphor in text analysis affords students a clear
overview of the key ideas in metaphor theory, as well as the necessary tools
to explore the field further.

Adopting a multi-disciplinary approach, the book provides a thorough
grounding in metaphor and word meaning, theories on the processing and
understanding of metaphorical language, and metaphor in other languages
and translation. Distinguished authors, Rosamund Moon and Murray
Knowles, draw on a wide selection of material to explore metaphor in
relation to text, discourse and society. Linguistic metaphor and literary
metaphor are examined across a range of contexts, such as politics, sport
and advertising, whilst literary metaphor is demonstrated through authentic
extracts from fiction and poetry. A final section covering non-verbal
metaphor looks at metaphor in art, cinema and music.

Featuring suggestions for further reading and an appendix for small-scale
research investigations on metaphor, this book will be invaluable to
undergraduate students of English Language, Linguistics and Literature.

Hbk: 978-0-415-27800-3
Pbk: 978-0-415-27801-0

Available at all good bookshops
For ordering and further information please visit:
www.routledge.com

Routledge Critical Thinkers

Series Editor: Robert Eaglestone, Royal Holloway, University of London

Routledge Critical Thinkers is designed for students who need an accessible introduction to the key figures in contemporary critical thought. The books provide crucial orientation for further study and equip readers to engage with each theorist's original texts.

The volumes in the Routledge Critical Thinkers series place each key theorist in his or her historical and intellectual contexts and explain:

- why he or she is important
- what motivated his/her work
- what his/her key ideas were
- what to read next and why.

- who and what influenced the thinker
- who and what the thinker has influenced

Featuring extensively annotated guides to further reading, Routledge Critical Thinkers is the first point of reference for any student wishing to investigate the work of a specific theorist.

'These little books are certainly helpful study guides. They are clear, concise and complete. They are ideal for undergraduates studying for exams or writing essays and for lifelong learners wanting to expand their knowledge of a given author or idea.' – Beth Lord, *THES*

'This series demystifies the demigods of theory.' – Susan Bennett, University of Calgary

Available in this series:

Louis Althusser by Luke Ferretter
Roland Barthes by Graham Allen
Jean Baudrillard by Richard J. Lane
Simone de Beauvoir by Ursula Tidd
Homi K. Bhabha by David Huddart
Maurice Blanchot by Ullrich Haase and William Large
Judith Butler by Sara Salih
Gilles Deleuze by Claire Colebrook
Jacques Derrida by Nicholas Royle
Michel Foucault by Sara Mills
Sigmund Freud by Pamela Thurschwell
Antonio Gramsci by Steve Jones
Stephen Greenblatt by Mark Robson
Stuart Hall by James Procter

Martin Heidegger by Timothy Clark
Fredric Jameson by Adam Roberts
Jean-François Lyotard by Simon Malpas
Jacques Lacan by Sean Homer
Julia Kristeva by Noëlle McAfee
Paul de Man by Martin McQuillan
Friedrich Nietzsche by Lee Spinks
Paul Ricoeur by Karl Simms
Edward Said by Bill Ashcroft and Pal Ahluwalia
Gayatri Chakravorty Spivak by Stephen Morton
Slavoj Žižek by Tony Myers
Theorists of Modernist Poetry: T. S. Eliot, T. E. Hulme, Ezra Pound by Rebecca Beasley

Available at all good bookshops
For further information on individual books in the series, visit:
www.routledge.com/literature/rct